Dedicated by
Ellen Kim & Anna Cho
May 05

D1784079

KOREAN HERITAGE

II

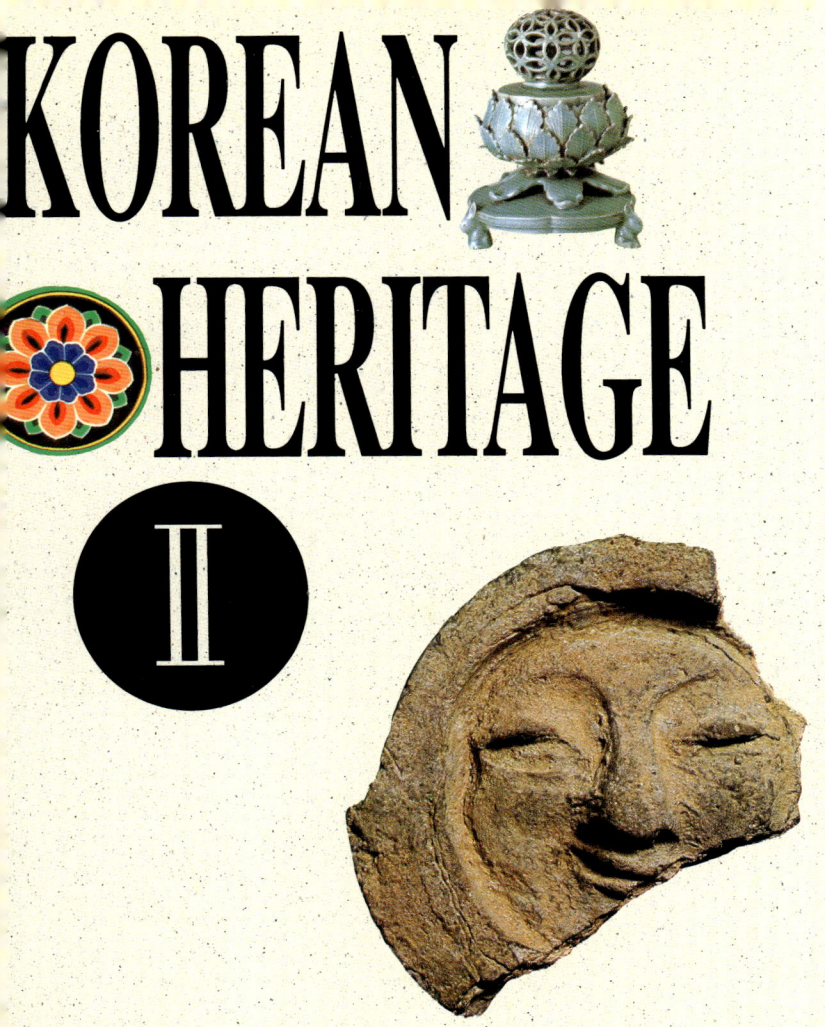

HOLLYM

Elizabeth, NJ · SEOUL

Copyright © 1996
by Korean Overseas Culture and Information Service

All rights reserved

First published in 1996
Second printing, 1998
by Hollym International Corp.
18 Donald Place, Elizabeth
New Jersey 07208 U.S.A.
Tel:(908)353-1655 Fax:(908)353-0255

Published simultaneously in Korea
by Hollym Corporation; Publishers
13-13 Kwanchol-dong, Chongno-gu
Seoul 110-111, Korea
Tel:(02)735-7551~4 Fax:(02)730-5149

ISBN 1-56591-078-8
Library of Congress Catalog Card Number:96-78905

Printed in Korea

Table of Contents

Traditional Musical Instruments

There are approximately sixty traditional Korean musical instruments that have been handed down through the generations, each boasting a long and rich history. They include the *kayagŭm* (12-string zither) and the *kŏmun-go* (six-string zither), both presumed to have originated before the sixth century.

Traditional Musical Instruments

There are approximately sixty traditional Korean musical instruments that have been handed down through the generations, each boasting of a long and rich history. They include the *kayagǔm* (12-string zither) and the *kǒmun-go* (six-string zither), both presumed to have originated before the sixth century; the three string and three bamboo instruments of the Unified Shilla Dynasty; court instruments of the Chosǒn Dynasty; and numerous others that are still being played.

Native or folk instruments played a major role in the development of music in Korea from early civilizations to the Unified Shilla Kingdom(668-935). The period of the Three Kingdoms (57 B.C.-A.D. 668) witnessed the first introduction of Central Asian instruments into the country. This, along with the subsequent import of Chinese instruments, most importantly from T'ang China during the late Unified Shilla period and from

Korean musical instruments have a long history and tradition. Shown here are musicians performing on court instruments.

Sung China during the Koryǒ (918-1392) period, sparked a significant rise in the number of available instruments. This in turn made it possible for musicians to experiment, thereby expanding the scope and depth of local music. With time, Chinese instruments imported during these periods were slowly integrated into local music, and by the time the Chosǒn Dynasty (1392-1910) was established, they had already become an integral part of Korean music. Traditional Korean instruments can be broadly divided into three groups: string, wind, and percussion instruments. Based on their function, they can further be divided into native (Hyang), T'ang (of Chinese origin), and court ceremonial instruments.

Kayagǔm:
The most representative instrument of Korea.

STRING INSTRUMENTS
1. Native Instruments

Kayagǔm (12-string zither) : The *kayagǔm* is the most representative instrument of Korea. Its origin can be traced back to the Kingdom of Kaya in the sixth century, when the Shilla Kingdom was ruled by King Chinhǔng. However, the actual production of the first *kayagǔm* is presumed to have been much earlier. The instrument is constructed with 12 strings supported by 12 moveable bridges. The *kayagǔm* can be divided into two groups according to the types of music played upon them. The *sanjo kayagǔm* is used in folk and improvisatory musical pieces such as *sanjo* (solo music with drum accompaniment) and *shinawi* (improvisational ensemble music). The *chŏng-ak kayagŭm* is used in chamber music such as *Yŏngsan Hoesang* (mass at the sacred mountain) or to accompany lyric songs.

Kŏmun-go (six-string zither): Along with the *kayagŭm*, the *kŏmun-go* is one of the most important Korean instuments. Instruments that appear to be early, primitive forms of the *kŏmun-go* have been discovered inside ancient Koguryŏ tombs in various locations. The *kŏmun-go* that is used today is constructed with six strings and 16 frets, and is played with a plectrum. It is used to accompany lyric songs as well as in chamber music and *sanjo* (solo music with drum accompaniment).

Kŏmun-go:
An important
Korean instrument.

2. T'ang Instruments
(Instruments of Chinese origin)

Haegŭm (two-string fiddle):
Although it was first imported
from China, the *haegŭm* has
since been fully absorbed into
the local culture. Today it is
popularly used in various
genres of Korean music. The
instrument is played by inserting
a resined bow between the two
strings and rubbing it against the
strings. It is currently used in
chŏng-ak (chamber music) and

Haegŭm

sanjo (solo music with drum accompaniment). In
particuar, the *haegŭm* is an indispensable part of *sam-
hyŏn yukkak*, the ensemble consisting of string and wind
instruments that is used to accompany dance.

Ajaeng (seven-string bowed zither) : The three types
of *ajaeng* are the *chŏng-ak ajaeng*, the *sanjo ajaeng*, and the
taejaeng. The *chŏng-ak ajaeng* is constructed with seven
strings and is used in T'ang music such as *Nagyangch'un*
(Spring in Loyang) and *Pohŏja* (Walking in the Void) as
well as in native music such as *Yŏ-millak* (Enjoyment
with the People) and *Chŏng-ŭp* (A song of Chŏng-ŭp
city). The *sanjo ajaeng* has eight strings and is used
exclusively in folk music such as *sanjo* and *shinawi*. The
taejaeng is a large *ajaeng* with fifteen strings. While once
widely used to play Chinese music during the Koryŏ
and Chosŏn Dynasties, the *taejaeng* is no longer in use.

Ajaeng concert (right).

3. Court Ceremonial Instruments

Kŭm (seven-stringed zither): The *kŭm* has seven strings and a base with thirteen marks inlaide with mother-of-pearl, which mark the place where to press down on the string. Used exclusively in court music ensembles during the Chosŏn Dynasty, the instrument is no longer used.

Sŭl (twenty-five string zither): This instrument has twenty five strings with 25 bridges. Along with the *kŭm*, the *sŭl* was used exclusively in court music ensembles, and like the former is no longer played.

4. Other Instruments

Yanggŭm (dulcimer): A European instrument that was imported from China during the 18th century, the yanggŭm has 14 quadruple brass strings stretched over and under two brass bridges. The instrument is played by tapping the strings with a small bamboo stick.

Taegŭm (left) and *sogŭm* (right).

WIND INSTRUMENTS
1. Native Instruments

Taegŭm (large transverse flute) : The *taegŭm* is one of three bamboo wind instruments of the Unified Shilla period. The type used during that period was the *chŏng-ak taegŭm*. Another type currently used today is the *sanjo taegŭm*. The *chŏng-ak taegŭm* has 13 holes and is typically used for chamber music and song accompaniment. While similar to the *chŏng-ak taegŭm* in overall construction, the *sanjo taegŭm* is slightly smaller in size and shorter in length. The two types of *taegŭm* differ in their application as well: *sanjo taegŭm* is used in *sanjo* (solo music with drum accompaniment) and *shinawi* (improvisational ensemble music) or to accompany folk songs and dance. The two types show a variation in pitch of a minor third when played with three holes.

Hyang-p'iri

Sogŭm (small flute) : The *sogŭm* is one of the three bamboo instruments along with the *taegŭm* (large flute) and the *chunggŭm* (medium-sized flute). While popularly used until the Chosŏn Dynasty, there are are no remaining relics or prototypes to verify the exact shape of the instrument. A model of the *sogŭm* was reconstructed based on existing documents, and this is the type that is currently being used.

Hyang-p'iri (Korean cylindrical oboe) : The *hyang-p'iri* has seven finger holes and is used to perform *chŏng-ak* (chamber music) such as *Yŏngsan Hoesang* and *Chŏng-ŭp*, and folk music including *sanjo* (solo music with percussion accompaniment) and wind orchestration.

Ch'ojŏk (grass flute) : Made from blades of grass, the *ch'ojŏk* was widely popular among the common folk of Korea.

2. T'ang Instruments (instruments of Chinese origins)

Tang-p'iri (Chinese oboe) : Shorter than *hyang-p'iri* but with a thicker cylinder, the current version of *tang-p'iri* has eight holes and is typically used to perform Chinese music.

T'ungso (vertical flute) : The two types of *t'ungso* are the *chŏng-ak t'ungso* and the folk *t'ungso*. The *chŏng-ak t'ungso* has nine holes and while widely popular until the Chosŏn Dynasty, it is no longer used. The folk *t'ungso* has five holes in all, one in the back, and four in the front. One has a reed membrane. The instrument is used in *shinawi* (improvisational ensemble music), *sanjo* (solo music with drum accompaniment), and the *Pukchŏng* lion dance.

T'aep'yŏngso (conical oboe) : The *t'aep'yŏngso* was imported from China in the late

T'ungso (left) and *tang-p'iri* (right).

T'aep'yŏngso

Yak (left)
and chŏk (right).

Tanso

So

fourteenth century during the late Koryŏ or early Chosŏn Dynasty. With eight finger holes, the instrument is played by inserting a reed in the blowhole. It is most widely used in *nong-ak* (farmers' music).

3. Court Ceremonial Instruments

Saeng (mouth organ), *U* (large mouth organ), and *Hwa* (small mouth organ) : The three mouth organs are similar in their construction and only differ in the number of pipes. The *saeng* has 17 pipes, the *hwa* has 13, and the *u*, the largest, has 36. The only one still in use is the *saeng* used to perform both Chinese and native music.

So (panpipes) : The three types are the 12-pipe, the 16-pipe, and the 24-pipe. The only one still being used in Korea is the 16-piped version, exclusively in court ceremonial music.

Hun (globular flute) : The *hun* is created from baked clay and has five holes in all. It is used exclusively in

Munmyo Cherye-ak (ritual music performed at Confucian shrines).

Chi (flute with mouthpiece) : The *chi* has five finger holes in all, one in the back and four in front. The intervals between the holes are irregular. The instrument is used exclusively in court ceremonial music.

Yak (small-notched flute) : Played vertically, the *yak* has three finger holes and is used in court music.

Chŏk (flute) : Played vertically, the *chŏk* has one blowhole and six finger holes and is used in court ceremonial music.

4. Other Instruments

Tanso (vertical flute): First played during the late Chosŏn Dynasty, the *tanso* has five finger holes. It is used in chamber music such as *Yŏngsan Hoesang* and also for solo perfomances.

Ching

Se-p'iri (slender cylindrical oboe): The *se-p'iri* is a slenderized version of the *hyang-p'iri* and has less volume. The instrument is used in orchestral music where the string section provides the core performance. It is also used in chamber ensemble music such as *Yŏngsan Hoesang* and in lyric songs, *kasa* (vernacular narrative verse), and *shijo* (short lyric songs).

PERCUSSION INSTRUMENTS

1. Native Instruments

Ching (large gong) : Made from brass and played with a mallet wrapped in cloth, the *ching* was originally used in military music. Currently, it is widely used in a variety of music including *ch'wit'a* (band music for royal processions), *nong-ak* (farmers' music), *musok* music (shaman ritual music), and Buddhist music.

Kkwaenggwari (small gong or hand gong) : Similar to the *ching* in its form and construction, the *kkwaenggwari* is smaller in size. Unlike the *ching,* it is played with a small unwrapped mallet and therefore creates a much sharper and high-pitched sound. The instrument is used in *nong-ak* (farmers' music) and *musok* music (shaman ritual music).

Kkwaenggari

Sori-buk

Changgo

P'ungmul-puk (folk drum) : this is mostly used in *nong-ak* (farmers' music) and unlike the *changgo* (hourglass-shaped drum), the materials used on both drumheads are identical. The instrument is played by striking the drumheads with a stick made from hard wood.

Sori-puk (vocal accompaniment drum) : A modified version of the *p'ungmul-puk*, the *sori-puk* is similar to the former in its shape and construction. However, the two differ in that the *sori-puk* has tiny metal tacks embedded around the rim of both drumheads. It is mostly used to accompany *p'ansori* (dramatic-epic-narrative singing).

P'ungmul Changgo (folk hourglass-shaped drum) : The *p'ungmul changgo* has wooden body with two drumheads made of hide. The instrument is played by striking the drum-heads with two sticks, one in each

P'ungmul, changgo, buk, sogo, kkwaenggari, ching.

hand. It is mostly used in *nong-ak* (farmers' music) and also as accompaniment to folk songs and *chapka* (folk ballads).

Pak

2. T'ang Instruments
(instruments of Chinese origin)

Pak (clapper) : The *pak* is constructed of six wooden slats which are spread apart and then struck together, creating a clapping sound. The instrument was used to perform Chinese music during the Koryŏ Dynasty, in court ceremonial music during the early Chosŏn Dynasty, and then in native music during the mid-

P'yŏn-gyŏng

Choson Dynasty. It is used today for *Munmyo Cherye-ak* (ritual music performed at Confucian shrines) and court orchestral music and dance accompaniment.

Changgo (hourglass-shaped drum) : According to existing documents, the *chŏng-ak changgo* has been used since the Koryŏ Dynasty. It has a wooden body and is widely used in both Chinese and native music.

3. Court Instruments

P'yŏnjong (bronze bells) and *T'ŭkjong* (single bronze bell) : The *p'yŏnjong* is constructed of two rows (top & bottom) with eight bells in each row. All the bells are identical in size and only differ in their thickness. The

Ch'uk

bells are played by striking them with a horn-tipped mallet held in the right hand. The instrument was first imported from Sung China during the Koryŏ Dynasty. The first domestic production of the *p'yŏn-jong* was under King Sejong during the Choson Dynasty. Today, it is used in both native and Chinese court music. The *t'ŭk-jong* has a single bronze bell and is used exclusively in court ceremonial music.

P'yŏn-gyŏng (stone chimes) and *T'ŭkkyŏng* (single stone chime) : The *p'yŏn-gyŏng* is constructed of two rows (top & bottom) with

eight L-shaped stones in each row. Imported from China as a court instrument with the *p'yŏnjong* during the Koryŏ Dynasty, the *p'yŏn-gyŏng* was first produced domestically under King Sejong during the Chosŏn Dynasty. Its uses are identical to the *p'yŏnjong*. The *t'ŭk-kyŏng* is a single L-shaped stone and is used exclusively in court ceremonial music.

Ch'uk (percussion instrument with a square wooden box and mallet) : The *ch'uk* is one of the instruments used to signal the beginning of a performance. Imported from Sung China during the Koryŏ Dynasty, it is today used exclusively in ritual music performed at the Confucian and Royal Ancestor Shrine ceremonies.

ŏ (tiger-shaped wooden instrument) : The *ŏ* is a tiger-shaped wooden instrument with 27 saw-toothed ridges on its back. The instrument is played by scraping the ridges with a bamboo stick. It is used to signal the end of a performance and is currently used in ritual music performed at Confucian shrines.

A drum processional performed at the 1988 Seoul Olympics.

Traditional Korean instruments can
be broadly divided into three
groups: string, wind, and percussion
instruments. Based on their function,
they can further be divided into folk,
T'ang, and court instruments.

Masks and
Mask-dance Dramas

Masks are called *t'al* in Korean, but they are also known by many other names such as *kamyŏn, kwangdae, ch'orani, t'albak* and *t'albagaji*. Korean masks come with black cloth in the back to secure them behind the heads and also to simulate black hair. *T'alch'um*, which literally means "mask dance," is not just a dance performed by masked dancers but is also drama with masked characters enacting persons, animals or supernatural beings.

Masks and Mask-dance Dramas

Masks are called *t'al* in Korean, but they are also known by many other names such as *kamyŏn*, *kwangdae*, *ch'orani*, *t'albak* and *t'albagaji*. Korean masks come with black cloth in the back to secure them behind the heads and also to simulate black hair. *T'alch'um*, which literally means "mask dance," is not just a dance performed by masked dancers but is also a drama with masked characters enacting persons, animals or supernatural beings.

Masks and mask dances developed in Korea as early as the Prehistoric age. The masks can be categorized in two kinds: religious masks and artistic masks. Some masks were enshrined in shaman shrines and revered with periodical offering rites. Other religious masks were used to expel evil spirits, like Pangsangshi, which until recently, were seen at the forefront of a funeral procession to ward off evil spirits. Artistic masks were mostly used in dance and drama.

Masks and mask dances date back to prehistoric times in Korea. Shown here are various masks used in the Kangnyŏng mask dance.

However, these also had religious functions to some extent.

Most Korean *t'al* are solid but some are partly moveable like the eyeballs of the Pangsang-shi mask, the mouth of the lion mask and the winking eyes of some masks in dance drama. Of special note are the masks featured in a mask-dance drama developed in the Hahoe region. They are made out of two pieces, with the chin coming in a separate piece and attached to the upper part with strings. They have a great advantage of expression.

T'al not only characterize their respective roles but also reflect the expressions and bone structures of Korean faces. Their shapes are grotesque and greatly exaggerated, and their colors are deep and bright. This is because *t'alch'um*, the mask dance drama, was usually performed at night in the light from wood fires. Masks less powerful in expression and color would have failed to deliver the themes of the drama. Religious masks and masks for daytime performances were much less vivid.

Masks are made of paper, wood, gourd and fur. Paper masks and gourd masks are prevalent, because they are simpler to make and also because they are

A mask for the monk in Hahoe *pyŏlshin-gut* mask dance (above).
Hahoe *pyŏlshin-gut* mask dance (left).

1

2

3

lightweight and thus conventient to dance with.

Red, black, white and other primal colors are favored for effective characterization of the masks. The colors also identify the sex and age of the characters. An old person's mask is black, whereas that of a young man is red and that of a young woman white. In the traditional philosophy of identifying colors with directions and seasons, the black stands for the north and winter whereas the red stands for the south and summer. In many of the *t'alch'um* dramas, the young man always wins over the old in a symbolic gesture of the summer triumphing over the winter. In this sense, *t'alch'um* is a vestige of fertility rites.

4

5

Korean masks are quite
striking in appearance
and vivid in color.

. Ch'wibari, an old
  bachelor (Pongsan
  mask drama).
. Somu, a young shaman
  (Yangju *pyŏlsandae*
  drama).
. Yŏnnip, a high monk
  (Songp'a *sandae* drama).
. Hongpaek yangban,
  red/white aristocrat
  (Kosŏng *ogwangdae*
  mask dance).
. Kakshi, a young woman
  (Hahoe *pyŏlshin-gut*
  mask dance).

Most of the masks depict human faces but some
represent deities, and there are also masks of animals,
real and imagined. An interesting feature is that the
masks of *yangban*, the upper class gentlemen, are
almost always deformed in one way or another with
harelips, sometimes cleaved in both upper and lower
lips, a lopsided mouth, a distorted nose or squint eyes
– a reflection of the commoners' hostility toward the
privileged class.

Mask-dance dramas are basically a folk art
naturally developed among the common people of
Chosŏn society(1392-1910). They vary slighty according to region and performer but they all share
fundamental charateristics. They are based on a sense
of rebellion felt by the common people toward the
reality of their lives. Their basic themes are exorcism
rites, ritual dances or biting satire and parody of

human weaknesses, social evils and privileged class. Like the folk literature of the time, it appeals to its audiences by ridiculing apostate Buddhist monks, decadent noblemen, and shamans. The conflict between an ugly wife and a seductive concubine is another popular theme.

The mask-dance drama consists of several acts, but they are quite different from the acts in modern plays. They are a loose presentation of several different episodes in an omnibus style. Because the lines of the actors have been passed on in oral tradition, they are quite flexible and subject to improvisation. The dance part also can be lengthened or shortened freely, so that

Yangju *pyŏlsandae* mask-dance drama. Masks are used to represe a variety of characters in the mask dance and to create a dramatic effect (previous page).

Mask dances were performed in a *madang* or outdoor arena.
Tongnae *tŭllolŭm* mask dance.

the entire performance can take anywhere between three or four hours to the whole night until daybreak.

With regional variations, the mask-dance drama was generally performed on the First Full Moon, Buddha's Birthday on the Eighth of the Fourth Moon, *Tano* Festival and *Ch'usŏk*. It was also performed at festive occasions of the state or at rituals to supplicate for rain.

Traditionally, Korean mask-dance drama was always performed outdoors. During Koryŏ and Chosŏn periods, it was performed on an improvised stage called *sandae* or up on a sloped incline so that the audience in their seats below could see well. There was

Koreans enjoy mask dances, which use a wide variety of masks. Masks are still made today.

a screened area used as a dressing room to the left of the stage and musicians sat to right of the stage. Actors were all males until *kisaeng*, female entertainers, joined them in modern times to take up the role of shamans and concubines.

Lively dance accompanied by vigorous music from three string and six wind and percussion instruments take up the major part of a mask-dance drama performance, with actors stopping to deliver their lines with a great deal of gesticulation. Many of the roles do not have any dialogue of their own but act in

ask dance, or *t'alch'um*, is form of folk drama enjoyed the common people. scene from the Pongsan ask dance (left).

pantomime, their extraordinarily stylized masks delivering the dramatic impact of their characters. The dance enlivens the drama and functions to round up each scene but is also performed without any regard to the progress of the plot.

The most remarkable feature of Korean mask-dance drama is the enthuisiastic participation of the audience. Toward the end of a performance there is little distinction between the actors and the audience as they join together in robust dance and bring it to a truly affirmative life-enhancing finale. In Korean mask-dance drama, the common people could vent their frustrations through comic dramatization and enliven their lives with a collective experience of ecatasy.

A mask dance, which is so rich in history, is performed in Taehang-no, an area of Seoul known as a gathering place for young people.

Korean masks can be categorized in two kinds: religious masks and artistic masks. Some masks were enshrined in shaman shrines and revered with periodical offering rites. Artistic masks were mostly used in dance and drama.

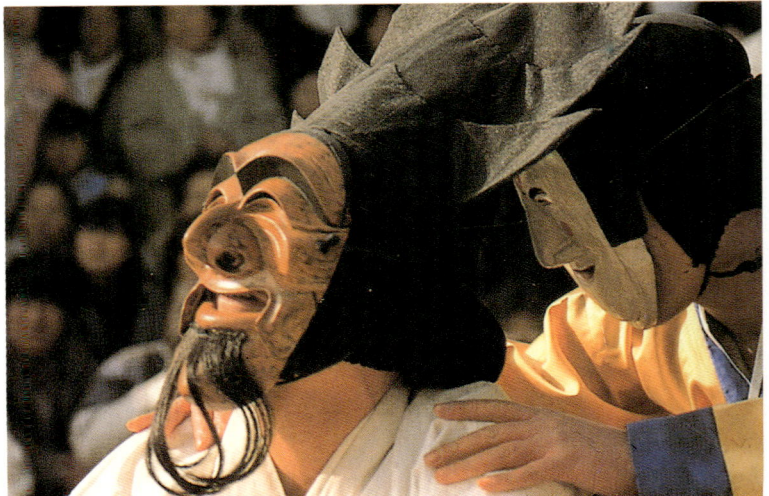

Seshi Customs

The expression "*seshi* customs" refer to ceremonial acts that are customarily repeated regularly during the year. *Seshi*, as days of festivity, act as a stimulus in life and accelerate the rhythm of the yearly life cycle so as to help one move on to the next step of the life cycle. *Seshi* customs are based on the lunar calendar. The sun was not believed to show any seasonal characteristics; the moon, on the other hand, was believed to show these seasonal characteristics well through its wane and unity with the passage of time.

Seshi Customs

The expression *seshi* customs refer to ceremonial acts that are customarily repeated regularly during the year. *Seshi*, as days of festivity, act as a stimulus in life and accelerate the rhythm of the yearly life cycle so as to help one move on to the next step of the life cycle.

Seshi customs are based on the lunar calendar. The sun was not believed to show any seasonal characteristics; the moon, on the other hand, was believed to show these seasonal characteristics well through its wane and unity with the passage of time. As a result, it was easy to observe and appropriately evaluate the seasonal change based on its changes.

Farming, however, was based on the twenty-four *chŏlgi* or "turning points." In summary, *seshi* customs followed the phases of the moon, while farming followed the 24 solar terms.

The *seshi* customs tended to deal with *shinkwan* (view of god), *chusulsŏng* (nature of sorcery), *chŏmboksok* (nature of fortune-telling), and *minsoknori* (folk

Sebae is a younger person bowing to an older person as the first greeting in the New Year.

games).

The gods included the *ilwŏlsŏng-shin* (god of the sun, moon, and stars) in the sky, the *sanchŏn-shin* (god of the mountains and rivers), the *yong-wang-shin* (the dragon king), the *sŏnang-shin* (a tutelary deity), and the *ka-shin* (god of home). These gods were waited upon for they were believed to be able to manipulate a person's luck and fortune. The days of performing sacrificial rites are festive days, and people pray for the gods' protection and conquest of demons on these days.

Ways of praying for good fortune, which were also acts of praying for the safety of the populace as a whole, included "selling away the heat," "nut cracking"(nuts eaten on the 15th day of the First Moon to guard oneself against boils for a year), "chasing away mosquitoes," "treading on the bridge," and "hanging a lucky rice scoop."

In an agricultural society such as Korea's, fortune-telling was performed to predict whether the forthcoming harvest would be good or bad, and depending on the prophecy, a good harvest was prayed for. Accordingly, in the first lunar month, when farming begins, fortune-telling was performed by listening for the sounds animals made and changes in the weather.

A lucky rice scoop with taffy, matches, or money inside was hung on the wall during the first ten days of the New Year.

If cows brayed or the weather was clear on the Lunar New Year's Day or on the 15th day of the First Moon, it was believed that a year of abundance was

Most Korean families hold an ancestor-memorial service on festive days, with items offered in sacrifice to the ancestral tablet.

ahead. When the sun was red, a drought was believed to be forthcoming. A northward wind meant a bad year, and the southward wind was believed to bring a year of abundance. In the case of folk games, whether a town's year would be good or bad was foretold via playing *yut* (a game using four wooden sticks) and a tug-of-war.

As a result, *seshi* customs could directly influence the policies of a nation, and at the same time, they were an important determinant factor in the characteristics of the Korean people and the structure of their consciousness. Presently, however, with the influence of Western culture and changing lifestyles, *seshi* customs are vanishing.

During the First Moon, New Year's Day–the biggest holiday of the year–and the 15th day were celebrated. On New Year's Day, Koreans enshrine their

In the first lunar month, a fire was started in the banks around paddy fields to chase away rats

ancestral tablet and hold a *ch'arye*. A *ch'arye* is the holding of an ancestor-memorial service on festive days, with things offered in sacrifice to the ancestral tablet.

Ordinarily ancestor-memorial services were held for ancestors up to four generations back; for ancestors further back than the fourth generation, ancestor-memorial services were held only once a year at their graves. Upon finishing the service at the graves, *sebae* (a formal bow of respect to one's elders) was performed. *Sebae* is a younger person's bowing to an older person as the first greeting at the new year. *Sebae* is done by kneeling down and bowing politely. After performing *sebae*, *sŏngmyo* was next. *Sŏngmyo* is a visit to the ancestal graves to bow and inform them of the new year. *Sŏngmyo* was a custom that was equal to doing *sebae* for living people; it was an absolutely necessary act of etiquette for descendants.

On New Year's Day and the first ten days of the first lunar month, there are various times when fortune is prayed for throughout the year. During the first ten days, each house bought a fortune mesh dipper and hung the dipper–with taffy, matches, or money in it–on the wall.

On the night before the 15th day of the First Moon, a scarecrow called a *cheung* was made and then thrown into a stream. This was to signify throwing away hapless fate and greeting a fortunate year. On the morning of the 15th day, drinking wine to "clear the ear" and cracking nuts were customs that were enjoyed.

By cracking and eating nuts with a hard shell (such as chestnuts, walnuts, pine nuts or ginko nuts), it was

T'ojŏngbigyŏl foretells one's fortune for the year and was very popular among the common people.

believed that one would not suffer from ulcers. By drinking wine to clear the ear, it was believed that one would receive good things to hear; in other words, one would hear good news often during that year.

One of the most well-known *seshi* customs was treading on a bridge before and after the 15th. When crossing a bridge in the evening, one crossed a bridge the number of times equal to one's age; by doing so, it was believed that one could stay healthy and not suffer from leg pains throught the year.

One of the *seshi* customs that cannot go unmentioned is fortunetelling. It was customary to attempt to foretell one's fortune or how good or bad the harvest for the year would be. Particularly, *t'ojŏngbigyŏl* was very popular among the common people because of its monthly explanation of fortune and its high accuracy.

In the first lunar month, each town performed *tongje. Tongje* refers to a ritual ceremony that was performed as a unit by a town. *Sanshin-je* (a ritual service for the god of mountains), *pyŏlshin-je* (a service for the special god), street ritual services, and a service for the dragon king are examples of *tongje*.

The end of the First Moon or the beginning of the Second Moon was called *Ipch'un* (the "onset of spring"). *Ipch'un* was believed to signal the beginning of the spring season. During this time, each house wrote a poem about the onset of the spring and pasted it on a pillar or on the front gate.

The first of the Second Moon was called *Yŏngdŭng* Day. *Yŏngdŭng*, the goddess of the wind, was believed to bring her daughter and daughter-in-law. If it was

In the first lunar month, families gathered around to play *yut* and hoped for continuing strong family ties.

Children have fun kite flying, playing shuttlecock games, and many other festive days (right).

windy, she was bringing her daughter; if it was rainy, she was bringing her daughter-in-law.

The 3rd day of the Third Moon was considered the day on which the swallows returned. As it became spring with its warming weather, people went out to the fields and ate a cake made in the shape of a flower. If sauce was made on this day, it was supposed to taste better; if a pumpkin was planted, many pumpkins would grow; and if any medicinal substances were taken, one was believed to live long without diseases.

The 8th day of the Fourth Moon is Buddha's birthday. It was also called Buddha's bathing day. On this day, people visited temples and prayed for the happiness of the dead while lighting lanterns.

The 5th day of the Fifth Moon is *Tano*. On this day, women washed their hair with iris and swung on a swing, while men wrestled in traditional Korean style *ssirŭm*.

Females washed their hair with iris and swung on a swing on the 5th day of the Fifth Moon, *Tano* (next page).

The 15th day of the Sixth Moon is called *Yudu*. On this day, people washed their hair in water that was flowing eastward, in the hope of eliminating bad happenings, and performed an ancestor-memorial service with freshly harvested fruit and rice cakes.

Between the Sixth and Seventh Moons, there was the midsummer heat. During this period, people sought mineral water, enjoyed river-fishing, and cooked very nutritious dishes, such as *samgye-t'ang* (a type of chicken soup with ginseng in it).

The 7th day of the Seventh Moon is *Ch'ilsŏk*, when Kyŏnwu(the Herdsman)and Chiknyŏ(the Vega) were believed to meet each other on a bridge. On this day, people dried their clothes and books under the sunshine. Wives and children performed a sacrificial ceremony at the well (for abundance of water) and *ch'ilsŏng-je* (an ancestor-memorial service for the Big Dipper God) to pray for the prosperity of their homes.

The 15th of the Seventh Moon is called *Paekchung* or *Chungwŏn*. Various fruits and vegetables are abundant during this time. *Paekchung* means serving 100 different things on the table for a memorial service. On the farmland, a ceremonial feast was prepared for the laborers in recognition of their work so they took a day off for an enjoyable time.

The 15th of the Eighth Moon is *Ch'usŏk*, Thanksgiving Day. Along with New Year's Day, *Ch'usŏk* (also called the Harvest Moon Festival) is the biggest holiday in Korea. With freshly harvested grains and fruits, ancestor-memorial services were performed, and visits to one's ancestors' graves were made. One of the dishes prepared for this day that cannot go unmentioned is *songp'yŏn* (a rice cake steamed on a layer of pine

needles). Inside *songp'yŏn*, freshly harvested sesame, beans, redbeans, chestnuts, or Chinese dates are stuffed.

On the night before *Ch'usŏk*, all the family members sat around and made *songp'yŏn*, looking at the round moon. Particuarly, single men and women tried their best in demonstrating their skills to make *songp'yŏn* as pretty as possible. That was because one was believed to be able to meet a good-looking spouse only if one was able to make good-looking *songp'yŏn*. During *Ch'usŏk*, people share wine and food, besides playing various kinds of fun games. Games such as *so-nori* (cow play), *kobuk-nori* (turtle play), *kanggangsuwŏllae* (a country circle dance), and *ssirŭm* (Korean wrestling) were performed, creating a lively atmosphere.

For *Ch'usŏk*, *songp'yŏn* is made with freshly harvested grains.

Freshly harvested grains and fruits were used during ceremonies to honor one's ancestors.

Kanggangsuwŏllae: Women gather to form a circle and dance under the full moon of *Ch'usŏk*.

The 9th day of the Ninth Moon is *chungyang-chŏl* or simply *chung-gu*. On *chung-gu*, people cooked pancakes with chrysanthemum leaves or made wine with mums. In groups, people went to the mountains or entered valleys to see the foliage, and enjoyed the day by eating food and drinking wine. Folks believed that beginning from *chung-gu*, mosquitoes were vanishing, swallows were flying south, and snakes and frogs began to enter the ground for hibernation.

The Tenth Moon was called *Sang-dal*, which means the moon shines the highest in the year. The moon during that month was considered sacred, and a ceremonial service was usually performed toward the sky. At home, people set the table with *siru-ttŏk* (a steamed rice cake) to calm the household god for peace in the household, and replaced the jar of the tutelary spirit (of house sites) with newly harvested grain.

The Elventh Moon was called *Tongjit-dal*; rice gruel (prepared with red beans mashed and strained) was made and served on the table of an ancestral tablet hall. The rice gruel was also thrown against the front gate and wall. This custom originated from trying to repel falsehood and was believed to keep away demons.

The last day (*Kŭmŭm*) of the last month was called *Chesŏk* or *Cheya*. It was a must for the people with debts to pay them off prior to the beginning of a new year. On this day, people caught birds, bowed in greeting to elders on that eve, performed *suse*, or cleaned the entire house. Bowing on that eve was intended to report to the elders that one had safely spent the year without any accident. *Suse* was lighting the house by a lighted

Tongji Puchŏk:
To chase away demons,
puchŏk (talisman) was
attached to front doors
and walls during *Tongji*
(the Eleventh Moon),
a time to end
the year and prepare
for the coming of
a new one.

torch at various places in the house, to symbolically prevent the approach of minor demons.

Also, while housewives prepared food to treat the New Year's guests, men cleaned in and outside the house. In other words, they were getting rid of the past year's minor demons and misfortunes and were preparing to begin a new year with a pure spirit.

Additionally, if one slept on this night, it was believed that one's eyebrows would turn white; therefore, it was a custom that people would stay up all night. When a sleeping child was found, his or her eyebrows would be painted by someone with white powder; the next morning people would tease the child by telling the child that his or her eyebrows' color had changed white.

Korea's *seshi* customs are part of old traditions. Those customs were rooted in life experiences. Therefore, *seshi* customs include an abundance of native wisdom.

Seshi customs could directly influence on the policies of a nation, and at the same time, they were an important determinant factor in the characteristics of the Korean people and the structure of their consciousness.

hamanism

...manism is a folk religion centered on ...elief in good and evil spirits who can ...ly be influenced by shamans. The ...man is a professional spiritual ...diator who performs rites. *Mudang*, ...Korean usually refers to female shamans, while male shamans are called *paksu*. ...en shamans dance, they enter a trance, and their souls depart their body for ... realm of the spirits. By falling into ecstasy, the shaman communicates ...ectly with the spirits and displays supernatural strength and knowledge as ...ir mouthpiece.

Shamanism

Shamanism is a folk religion centered on a belief in good and evil spirits who can only be influenced by shamans. The shaman is a professional spiritual mediator who performs rites. *Mudang*, in Korean usually refers to famale shamans, while male shamans are called *paksu*.

When shamans dance, they enter a trance, and their souls depart their body for the realm of the spirits. By falling into ecstasy, the shaman communicates directly with the spirits and displays supernatural strength and knowledge as their mouthpiece. The shaman plays the role of an intermediary between man and the supernatural, speaking for the humans to deliver their wishes and for the spirits to reveal their will.

The extraordinary gifts of the shaman allows him or her to be naturally distinguished from others in society. The belief that the shaman communicates with the spirits gives that person authority. In ancient

When shamans dance, they communicate directly with the spirits and, in turn, the spirits, through the shaman, reveal their will.

societies, probably from time of tribal states, the shaman assumed the role of a leader as his or her supernatural powers contributed to the common interest of the community. As the possessor of transcendental abilities which were beyond the capacity of ordinary human beings, the shaman may be defined by the following characteristics:

First, the shaman has to have experienced the torture of the spirits by resisting being chosen for the vocation, which is manifested in the form of illness. The supernatural abilities of the shaman result from being the choice of the spirits. The illness breaks the resistance of the shaman candidate and the person has to accept the vocation.

Second, the shaman should be capable of officiating at rites in which they are believed to communicate with the spirits. The rites constitute an essential religious expression in shamanism.

Third, the shaman needs to be recognized as a religious leader with the ability to satisfy the spiritual requirements of the community.

Fourth, the shaman has to serve and assist specific spirits. This indicates that the shaman has experienced and accepted specific spirits at the stage of initiation.

A great variety of spirits are worshiped in the pantheon of shamans, such as the mountain spirit, the seven star spirit, the earth spirit and the dragon spirit. In addition to these spirits in nature, the shaman may also serve the spirits of renowned historical figures including kings, generals and ministers.

Shamans are divided largely into two types according to their initiation process–those who are

A *paksu mudang* performs a ritual to worship the *changgun shin* (a spirit of a general).

hamanism is depicted in
"Munyŏdo," a painting by
hin Yun-bok. Chosŏn
ynasty.

chosen by the spirits and those who inherit the vocation from their ancestors.

The shamans who are chosen by the spirits are endowed with supernatural powers to heal and to divine. They communicate with the spirits and speak for them in rites. The costumes used by these possessed shamans vary widely, reaching some 12 to 20 kinds, representing the various spirits they embody. Percussion instruments are played in fast, exciting rhythms to accompany the shaman as she or he falls into ecstasy by dancing.

Shamans of this type experience without fail the so-

called *shinbyŏng*, the illness resulting from resisting the call of the spirits, as an unavoidable process of initiation. The shaman candidate usually faints, has visions, and similar symptoms. Then, in a vision or a dream, the spirit who has chosen them appears and announces their being chosen, a call nesessary for shamans to acquire their powers.

The illness will cause the future shaman to suffer for months, or perhaps for years. Statistics say that the illness lasts about eight years on the average, but in some cases, it may last as many as 30 years. In an extremely unstable psychological state bordering lunacy, the person can hardly eat and sometimes roams around in the fields and in the mountains. The illness, which defies modern medicine, disappears all of a sudden when the person finally gives way to the compulsion and becomes a shaman.

Then an initiation rite is held under the guidance of a senior shaman assuming the role of a godmother or a godfather. The novice shaman learns all the necessary skills of a professional shaman from the senior shaman before practising on his or her own. The apprenticeship lasts for about three years in most cases though it may vary depending on individual talent.

Those who become shamans by inheritance do not possess transcendental powers, and their role is restricted mostly to the performance of rites. The rites they officiate at do not involve ecstasy for communion with the supernatural, and no specific spirits are worshiped. These shamans do not keep altars, and for each rite they set up a sacred passageway for the descending spirits. During a rite, the shaman does not

e of the spirits
rshipped by shamans,
anggun shin.

embody the spirits but takes on a separate role.

The hereditary shamans use simple costumes of two or three kinds. But they use more colorful music of not only percussion but also string and wind instruments as well. Both the music and the dance are much slower than those performed by the "possessed" shamans.

Rites are performed for various purposes in shamanism, a religious phenomenon with deep roots in folk traditions. The rituals are divided largely into those performed for the guardian spirits of the house and the family, those for the tutelary spirits of the community and those for the deities of the universe.

First, the rites are performed frequently to invoke happiness. In ancient times, shaman rites were performed at all levels of society ranging from the royal household down to remote villages. Historical

Percussion instruments are generally used during rites (left). Shamans use diverse tools during rituals; various swords to represent the authority of spirits, fans, flags of five colors, old coins and cases for bamboo fortune sticks, etc (right).

records say that the court of the Koryŏ Dynasty set up 10 state shrines to perform rites to invoke peace and prosperity for the nation. Shamans danced and played music at these shrines for national well-being. Private rites were observed by aristocrats and commoners as well to pray for happiness in the family and in the village. These developed into communal rites and festivals in later years.

Second, shaman rites are purported to cure illness. Ancient people believed illness was caused by the spirits, which only the shamans could control. They even believed that the houses of the shamans were safe from the spirits causing illness, so, when epidemics spread, they took refuge at their houses.

When dangerous epidemics spread, the royal court invited shamans to perform rites to expel the evil spirits. At private homes, rites were performed frequently to chase away the smallpox spirit, called *mama* (lord) or *sonnim* (guest), both implying that it was an object of fear.

Third, shaman rites are performed to escort the soul of a dead person to heaven. Shaman rites in Korea are not only intended to appease the soul of a deceased person but also to unleash the baleful elements which brought about the death. This allows the soul of the victim to find peace in heaven and to never bring bad fortune to the living. Particularly, deaths from illness or accidents were considered to need the rites in order to guide the wandering and unhappy souls of the dead to heaven.

Shaman rites are classified into three kinds based on their style. The simplest form is offering prayers while rubbing one's palms. Rites of the possessed shamans are characterized by an ecstatic state in which the shaman is deified or embodies the spirits. Rites of the hereditary shamans also involve communion with the supernatural but the shaman and the spirits keep their separate identities.

In the shamanistic world view, human beings have both a body and a soul, or even several souls. The soul, which provides the vital force of life for the body, never perishes. After the body dies, the soul lives forever in the after world, or is reborn in a new body.

Shamanism classifies souls into those of living

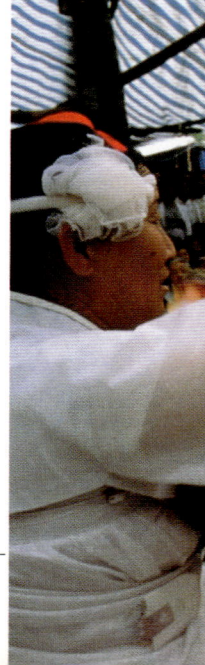

Kangshinmu ("possessed" shaman) refers to a person who became a shaman because he or she was chosen by the spirits (above). *Sesŭpmu* (hereditary shaman) is one who has inherited the vocation from their ancestors (below).

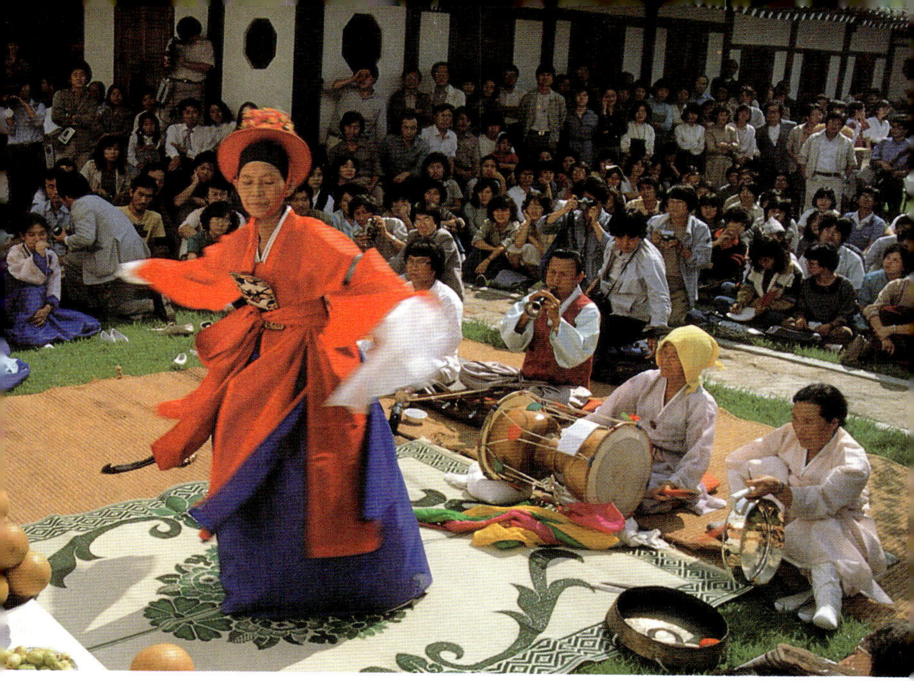

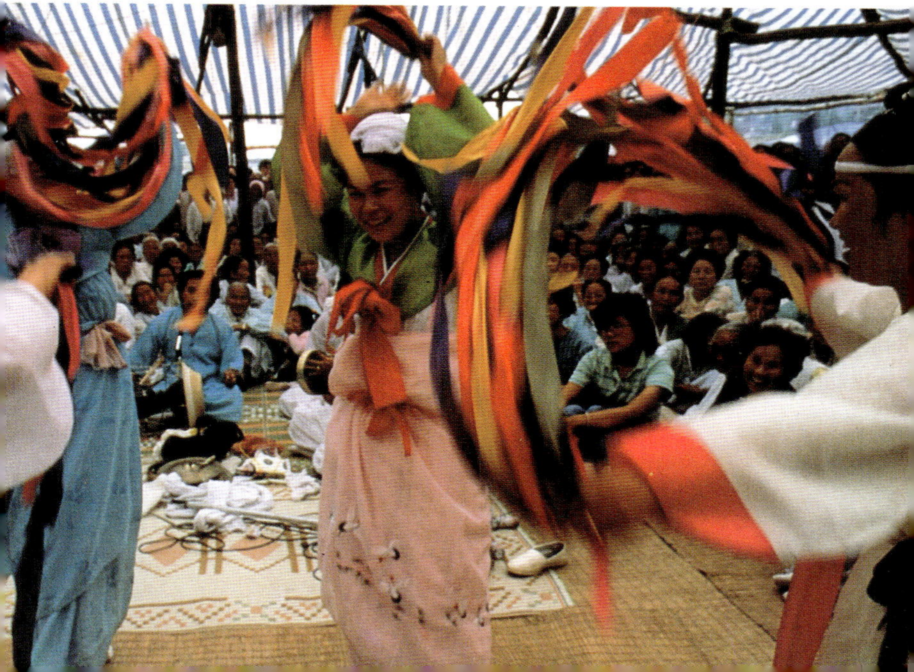

persons and those of dead persons. The souls of dead persons are personified, too. These souls are believed to be formless and invisible but omnipotent, floating around freely in the void with no barriers of time or space.

The shaman needs to serve and assist specific spirits. They are the spirits in nature and the spirits of renowned historical figures. A table prepared by a shaman for the *changgun shin* (previous page). Shamanist rituals involve experiences of ecstasy through dance. The influence of shamanism can be found in Korean modern dance (right).

The belief that the shaman
communicates with the spirits gives
that person authority.

Rites of Passage

An individual encounters many different stages in the course of life. A child grows up to become an adult, gets married, raises a family, becomes old and after death is mourned by his/her offspring. In Korea, the stages that an individual goes through in life and the accompanying changes in his/her social status have significant meaning.

Rites of Passage

An individual encounters many different stages in the course of life. A child grows up to become an adult, gets married, raises a family, becomes old, and after death is mourned by his/her offspring. In Korea, the stages that an individual goes through in life and the accompanying changes in his/her social status have significant meaning. The confusion that is likely to follow such changes is taken in stride through a series of rites of passage that are collectively called *Kwanhon sangje* (coming-of-age, marriage, funeral, ancestor worship).

In the Confucian society of traditional Korea, the coming-of-age rite signaled that the individual was officially a responsible member of society. Marriage reaffirmed the importance of the family as the basic unit of society. The funeral rites to mourn the passing of a family member and to overcome the resulting crisis in family life were austere and complex. The ancestral rite to pay homage to the family's forebears

A Korean traditional wedding ceremony was held according to a set procedure.

was aimed at strengthening
unity and harmony among
family members and rela-
tives.

A *kat* was placed on
a boy's head when
he reached twenty
and became an adult.

The Confucian coming-of-
age rite, transforming a child
into an adult, was simple. For
the boy, it consisted of tying
his long hair into a topknot,
and bestowing a *kat* (tradi-
tional cylindrical Korean hat made of horsehair) on the
boy's head. The ceremony was performed when he
reached his twentieth birthday. For the girl, it involved
rolling her braided hair into a chignon and fixing it
with a long ornamental hairpin called a *pinyŏ* when she
reached her fifteenth birthday.

Among commoners, the rite, as sponsored by the
village *ture* (farming cooperative), tested the boy's
physical strength by having him lift a designated rock.
If the boy proved his strength, he was considered
worthy of his mettle, and thus an adult.

Marriage in Korea was traditionally decided by the
senior elders of the two
families, and the cere-
mony was per-
formed in

Pinyŏ was used for the first time to fix the girl's hair
on her fifteenth birthday (above).
The Confucian coming-of age rite signaled that the individual
was officially a responsible member of society (right).

accordance with prescribed formalities: once a matchmaker confirmed the agreement to marriage by both families, the bridegroom's family sent to the bride's family a letter indicating the groom's *saju p'alcha* ("four pillars," indicating the year, month, day, and hour of his birth, which are presumed to determine his fate and fortune). The bride's family decided on a wedding date and notified the other side, which was followed by the groom's family sending the ceremonial wedding dress and gifts to the bride.

Unlike in China or Japan, the wedding ceremony in Korea is traditionally performed at the bride's home. It begins with the groom presenting a pair of wooden geese to the bride's family. The groom then exchanges bows with the bride, and shares with her a drink of wine in a gourd dipper. After the ceremony, the newlyweds usually spend two or three days with the bride's family (but the stay was known to last as long as a year in some cases). Upon arriving at the groom's house, the bride offers deep bows and gifts to the groom's parents and relatives, which symbolize the beginning of her new life with her in-laws.

Traditional marriage, modern style.

The traditional Korean wedding ceremony was an honoring of the ancestors and a public display that continuity in the family line was assured. The family, which was created by the marriage, was considered the basis of social life, and it was a social obligation of the partners to the marriage to lead prolific and prosperous lives.

Meanwhile, the funeral rites to mourn the loss of a loved one were played out in complex formalities and procedures in traditional Korea. During the Chosŏn

period when Confucianism took root as the guiding moral and ethical system, funerals became particularly elaborate as an undertaking not limited to the immediate family but extended to the entire clan. Much of this tradition is still practiced today.

The purpose of a funeral service is to enable the bereaved family to overcome the sense of loss and fear and to smooth the transition to daily life without the deceased. The passing of one's parents is always particularly sad. For Koreans, the funeral–including the monetary contributions to the deceased family and the assigned duties and roles–symbolizes the full extent and nuances of the family bonds.

Traditionally, mourning lasted for two years, following a strict set of protocol involving a series of prayer rites interspersed over the period. The intervals between the prayers, including the offering of food to the deceased and rites to conclude the burial, would be lengthened over time until at the end of the two years, the principal mourners would doff their ceremonial garb and other tokens of bereavement and return to their normal daily lives.

The various steps and rites that make up a complete funeral and period of mourning are as follows:

1. *Ch'ojong* (initial departing):

Preparations are made for the hour of death and immediately thereafter. The family discusses such matters as invocation of the spirit of the deceased, dressing the corpse, assignment of roles and preparation of the casket. As death nears, a piece of cotton is placed on the nose of the dying body, to determine the moment breathing ceases. When the breathing stops, *kok*, the ceremonial wailing begins. The deceased is undressed, and the clothes are taken to the roof of the house, where the outer garment is waved toward the north, and the name of the deceased is called out three times.

The garments are then collected in a basket and placed next to the spot where the tablets of the family's ancestors are kept. A curtain of folding screen is drawn around the deceased. The corpse is placed on a board with the head pointing south. The mouth is left open, and the feet are straightened and fixed to a wooden board. Meanwhile, a table of food is prepared for the

The *manjang* (funeral ode) and flower *sangyŏ* (funeral bier) lead the funeral procession

messenger from the other world.

2. *Sŭp* (cleansing the corpse):

The corpse is washed and dressed. The fingernails and toenails are clipped, and the hair neatly combed. The loose strands of hair and nail clippings are kept in a small pouch. The undergarments go on first, followed by the socks.

Rice is fed into the mouth three times, along with three pieces each of money and beads. After the eyes are covered, the ears stuffed, and a band tied around the waist, the hands are wrapped and a sheet is placed over the corpse.

3. *Soryŏm* (wrapping the corpse):

The day after *sŭp* is performed, the outer clothing and a cover with which to wrap the corpse is laid out. The upper garment goes on first, followed by the lower one. The other pieces are added on to form a square, which is followed by the final cover.

4. *Taeryŏm* (placing the corpse in the coffin):

Before placing the corpse in the coffin, ash is sprinkled on the bottom of the coffin. A thin board with seven holes standing for the seven stars that make up the Big Dipper is put in place, followed by a mattress. The corpse is set in placed, the empty space being filled with old clothing of the deceased. The coffin is shut and fixed with nodeless nails, and then covered with the final wrapping.

5. *Sŏngbok* (dressing oneself):

There is a set of procedures the immediate family and close relatives must follow in wearing their mourning clothing. It includes the duration for which

Generally, the eldest son becomes the principal mourner.

the clothing must be worn: three years, one year, nine months, five months, or three months depending on one's relation to the deceased. The practice calls for up to the third cousins of the deceased to dress for mourning. Once everyone is dressed, the principal mourner, typically the eldest son of the deceased, offers a prayer to indicate that all have gathered.

6. *Chosang* (visitors paying homage):

Visitors come to express their condolences to the bereaved family. At this time, when the principal mourner wails, the visitor is expected to do the same before the altar of the spirit of the deceased. He then bows twice before dismissing himself. An exchange of bows with the principal mourner completes the act of paying homage.

7. *Munsang* (hearing of death):

Sometimes the principal mourner is away when a death in the family occurs. If it is the death of a parent, he must first wail, change his clothes and start out on the trip home. During the journey, and when home finally appears in his sight, he may wail again. Upon arriving home, he bows twice before the deceased. After changing into his mourning garb, he wails again.

8. *Ch'ijang* (preparing the grave site):

Once the grave site is determined, the hollow must be dug and the tablet prepared.

9. *Ch'ŏn-gu* (removing the corpse):

The corpse, which is carried to the ancestral shrine, is symbolically reported to the ancestors, and then brought back to the house and placed at the center of the open space.

10. *Palin* (starting of funeral procession):

The corpse is removed from the house and placed on the funeral bier. Before the procession starts, a ceremony is performed. When the bier passes by the home of a friend of the deceased, the friend is expected to stop the procession and offer a *noje* (street rite).

11. *Kŭpmyo* (arrival at the grave site):

This refers to the process from the arrival of the procession at the grave site to the burial of the corpse.

12. *Pan-gok* (wailing upon return):

Upon returning home from the grave site with the tablet, the mourners wail again.

13. *Uje* (rites to console the deceased):

To comfort the spirit of the deceased, which may be wandering around aimlessly after the burial of the body, sacrificial rites are performed three times.

14. *Cholgok* (end of wailing):

The day after the third *Uje*, about 100 days after the death, a ceremony is performed to mark the formal end of wailing.

15. *Puje* (placing the tablet):

The tablet of the deceased is placed along with those of his/her ancestors.

16. *Sosang* (small service):

This memorial rite is held thirteen months after the death, to mark the first anniversary.

17. *Taesang* (large service):

This memorial rite is held twenty-five months after the death, to mark the second anniversary.

18. *Tamje:*

This memorial rite is held two month after *Taesang*.

19. *Kilche* (good rite):

This memorial rite is held in the month following

Tamje.

In addition to these elaborate funeral rites, Koreans have handed down a rich tradition of ancestral memorial rites through numerous rituals that honor the spirits of their ancestors and seek their blessings for the living descendants. The rites provide a connection between the dead and the living. Unlike the people of the West, Koreans of old believed that the world after death is not entirely separate from the present world but exists on the same continuum. To worship one's ancestors, and to give them continuity in life through offspring was considered the primary responsibility of filial children. To this day, devout Confucianists offer services for their parents, grandparents, great-grandparents, and great-great-grandparents on the anniversaries of their deaths. In addition, the ancestors are offered a *tarye* (tea rite) on the morning of folk

At the grave, the casket is buried and the bier is burnt.

holidays such as the Lunar New Year's Day. They are also offered a *shije* (time rite) at their grave sites. It is sometimes said that these rites breed clannishness and exclusivity; however, they also nurture intergenerational bonding and pride.

The *shije*, or ancestor memorial rite, is held at graves of four generations of ancestors.

In the Confucian society of traditional Korea, the funeral rites to mourn the passing of a family members and to overcome the resulting crisis in family life were austere and complex.

Korean Ginseng

Ginseng is a medicinal plant with wondrous powers. Although it grows in other countries as well, it is widely cultivated in Korea where the climate and soil produce the world's finest. It is a perennial herb that belongs to the "Araliaceae" family. Scientifically it is known as Panax schinseng Nees. A ginseng plant usually grows to be about 60cm tall.

Korean Ginseng

Ginseng is a medicinal plant with wondrous powers. Although it grows in other countries as well, it is widely cultivated in Korea where the climate and soil produce the world's finest. It is a perennial herb that belongs to the *Araliaceae* family. Scientifically it is known as *Panax schinseng Nees*.

A ginseng plant usually grows to be about 60cm tall. The subterranean stem is short, and stands either straight or slightly tilted. The root looks similar to that of a Chinese bellflower, with a single stalk growing out the stem. Three or four leaves grow at the end of the stalk. Light-green flowers blossom in April. When the flowers wither away, they are replaced by round, reddish fruit.

To distinguish it from ginseng grown in other parts of the world, Korean-grown ginseng is specifically called "Koryŏ ginseng," named after the ancient dynasty of Koryŏ from which the nation's current English name "Korea" is derived. Even in the old days, Korean ginseng used a different Chinese character for

Korean ginseng is the world's finest in quality and effectiveness.

"*sam*" (meaning ginseng):"參" was used for other types, while "蔘" was reserved for Korean ginseng.

Ginseng grown in the wild, deep in the mountains, is known as *sansam* (mountain ginseng). It is, however, found only rarely, and cultivation meets nearly all of the demand these days. Koryŏ ginseng's reputation began with *sansam*. In the old day, the search for it was almost a spiritual endeavor for those dwelling in the nation's mountainous regions. Even today, there are those who spend their lives wandering around deep valleys for the mystical plant. They are known as *shimmani* or *shimmemani* (both mean "gatherer of wild ginseng").

The territory of the kingdom of Koguryŏ(37 B.C.-A.D.668) extended north to the Liaotung region of China, Manchuria, and the coastal provinces of Siberia.

A *shimmani* is showing a *sansam* found deep in the mountains (above). *Sansam*, known as a mysterious cure, is also frequently depicted in paintings portraying immortals (right).

Wild ginseng grew in these regions as well as on the Korean Peninsula. Koguryŏ had a virtual monopoly on the supply of ginseng in those days. Since then, the preeminence of Koryŏ ginseng has continued to this day. In modern times, Koreans have developed unique cultivation, treatment, and merchandising techniques to preserve the nation's honor as the home of the world's finest ginseng. The constitution of ginseng changes with climate and soil conditions. Thus, the quality of Koryŏ ginseng is different from those of other types, so much so that it has its own scientific name.

Ginseng grown in America is called American, western, *Kwangdong, Hwagi*, or *P'o ginseng* ; *Panax quinquefolium* Linne is the scientific term. Japan's ginseng is *Panax japonicum* C.A. Meyer, and China's *Panax notoginseng* (Burk) F.H. Chen. They all belongs to the *araliaceae* family, but are fundamentally different from Koryŏ ginseng. Siberian ginseng, which is widely sold in Europe and America these days, also belongs to the same family, but not to the *Panax* (ginseng) genus. It is the root of a shrub, known by its scientific name, *Eleutherococcus senticosus* Maxim. Ginseng is very sensitive to climate and soil, and is thus extremely difficult to cultivate. Different locations of cultivation make for vastly different shapes, qualities, and medicinal powers. Hence, ginseng grown in other countries can hardly match Korean ginseng.

Ginseng cultivation in Korea began centuries ago, according to historical materials found in Korea and elsewhere. *Pents'ao kangmu* (Korean: *Ponch'o kangmok*;

Ginseng fruit (above and ginseng farm (right

Encyclopedia of Herbs), 52 volumes on the medicinal properties of plants, minerals and insects, was begun in 1552 and published in 1590 by a Ming Chinese scholar named Li Shizhen. It details how people at that time grew and traded ginseng. Some ancient Korean compilations of folk wisdom and mythology indicate that even as early as the fifth century, ginseng had begun to be cultivated from strains collected in the wild. Another record refers to the existence of ginseng cultivation in the eighth century during the Shilla Kingdom (57B.C.-A.D.935). Still another states that ginseng cultivation was widely practiced in the days of King Kojong (1213-1259) during the Koryŏ Dynasty.

Taken together, these materials indicate that ginseng cultivation originated in the area around Mt. Mohusan in the township of Tongbok in an area which is now a part of Chŏllanam-do province. It was quickly picked up by the enterprising merchants of Kaesŏng, the capital of Koryŏ, who introduced *Tongbok* ginseng to the residents of the capital, and the area around Kaesŏng quickly became the center of ginseng cultivation.

Korea's expertise in cultivation, coupled with perfect weather and soil conditions, has made Korean ginseng a prized product on the global market. The following are the optimum conditions for ginseng cultivation.

1. Temperature: 9-13.8℃ yearly average; 20-25℃ during the summer. Physiological defects appear at around 35℃.

2. Precipitation: 700-2,000mm yearly (1,100-

nseng, grown with
ard work and devotion,
traded in the market.

Ginseng is cleaned at
a ginseng processing
factory (above).
Ginseng is dried
in the sun (front).

1,300mm optimum). Relatively small snowfall desirable.

3. Lighting: diffuesd lighting at 1/8 to 1/13 of the strength of natural outside light. Direct sunlight is detrimental to ginseng.

4. Soil: sandy top soil and clay deep soil with plenty of potassium.

5. Location: 5-15^0 slope in north/northeastern direction. (Or level land that drains well)

6. Other conditions that simulate the environment for ginseng grown in the wild, such as a thick accumulation of decaying foliage. Extensive use of chemical fertilizers makes the soil unnatural and thus unfit for ginseng.

By nature, the climate and soil of Korean Peninsula meet all of the above conditions. Thus, with the exception of Chejudo Island, ginseng can be grown in

International ginseng symposiums are frequently held in Korea, the leading exporter of ginseng.

almost all regions of the country.

The medicinal powers of ginseng are extensively discussed in numerous historic materials. In *Shennung pents'ao ching* (Korean: *Shinnong Ponch'ogyŏng*; Shen Nung's Pharmacopoeia), China's oldest written book on herbs, it is noted that ginseng protects the digestive system, calms the nerves, clears the eyes, and, if taken over a long period of time, makes the body light and agile.

Ginseng is used as a restorative or tonic, rather than as a cure for a particular illness. Traditional East Asian medicine officially lists the following effects of ginseng: strengthening of organs; stimulation of the heart; protection of the stomach and enhancement of stamina; and calming of nerves. As such, it is routinely prescribed to people with weak digestive systems and poorly functioning metabolisms. People with stomach discomfort, chronic indigestion, heartburn, emesis, and poor appetite can greatly benefit from ginseng.

Scientific research on the effects ginseng took off in the 1950s in both pharmaceutical and clinical studies, unveiling the mystery that had surrounded the plant for thousands of years. Korean scholars have made great contributions to the scientific inquiries into ginseng. They have consolidated the nation's reputation as the home of ginseng in every aspect–cultivation, treatment and merchandising, and even research.

Acccording to existing studies, the primary ingredient that gives ginseng its medicinal quality is saponin, which reduces fatigue, enhances the body's productivity, stimulates the development of sexual glands and brings down the blood sugar level. In late theoretical analyses, ginseng's basic medical action is presumed to be that of an adaptogen, enhancing the overall resistance of the boby and facilitating its normalization and recovery from a state of illness. More specifically, ginseng facilitates the production of glucocorticoid, an adrenocortical hormone, strengthening the ability of the adrenal cortex to deal with various kinds of stress to the body.

World class ginseng tea, ginseng capsules, and other ginseng products.

By stimulating the cerebral cortex and the choline, ginseng also brings down blood pressure, facilitates breathing, reduces excess sugar in the blood, assists the actions of insulin, increases red blood cells and hemoglobin, and strengthens the digestive tract. Active research is underway to prove that ginseng also facilitates the formation of bio protein and DNA, and suppresses cancer.

Indeed, science is confirming the age-old belief that ginseng is the elixir of life. Thus, ginseng is a central ingredient in numerous prescriptions in trational East Asian medicine. In Korea, where its wondrous powers were accepted long before modern science came into existence, it is also drunk as a tea and a liquor.

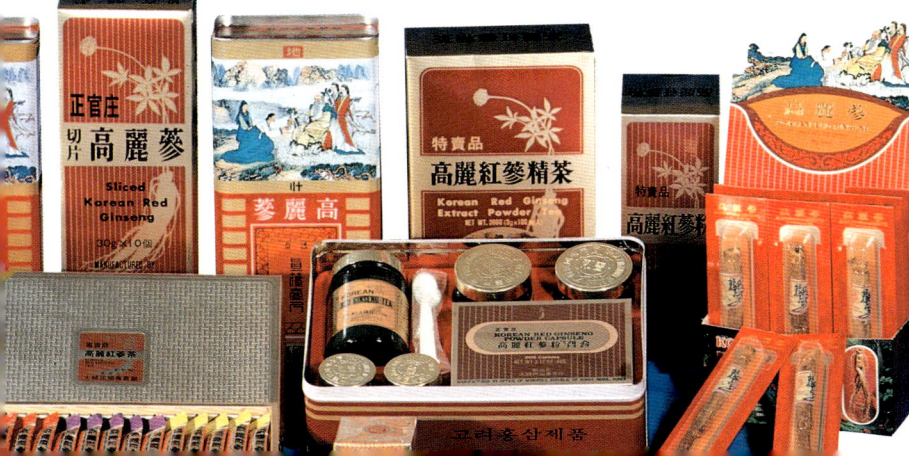

Ginseng is very sensitive to climate and soil, and is thus extremely difficult to cultivate. Different locations of cultivation make for vastly different shapes, qualities, and medicinal powers.

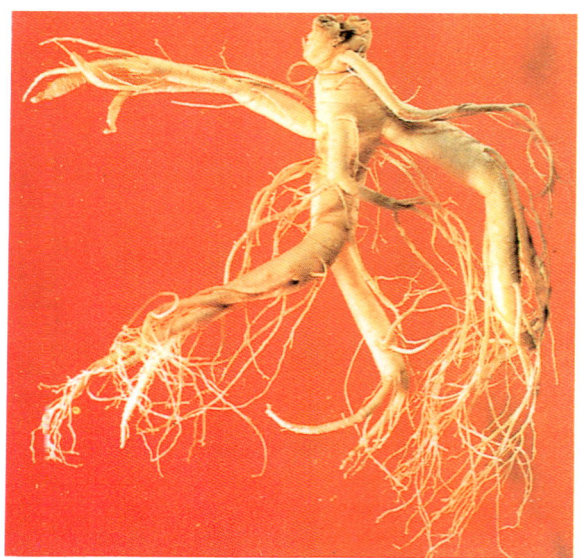

Kimchi

Kimchi is famous throughout the world as the traditional Korean pickled vegetable dish. Not only is kimchi rich in various nutrients, but the science of preparing kimchi makes it a very unique food indeed. The humna body requires the vitamins and minerals abundant in vegetables, but unlike grains, vegetables do not keep long. Of course, vegetables can be dried for preservation, but they tend to lose flavor and nutritional value over time.

Kimch'i

Kimch'i is famous throughout the world as the traditional Korean pickled vegetable dish. Not only is kimch'i rich in various nutrients, but the science of preparing kimch'i makes it a very unique food indeed.

The human body requires the vitamins and minerals abundant in vegetables, but unlike grains, vegetables do not keep long. Of course, vegetables can be dried for preservation, but they tend to lose flavor and nutritional value over time.

From ancient times, Koreans developed methods of perserving by salting or pickling vegetables with *chang* (a paste derived from soybean), vinegar, and other spices, and in the process developed a wholly new taste and smell.

Early Koreans would vigorously rub salt into the vegetable and preserve it in salt water or salt it again later. Depending on the time lapse between the first and second process, the natural juices of the vegetable would be released. These juices, mixed with the salt, would form a solution in which the vegetable was

There are numerous kinds of kimch'i, the traditional Korean pickled vegetable dish famous throughout the world.

steeped.

Otherwise, the vegetable would be suspended in liquid as in *tongch'imi*, sliced radish in a refreshing salty liquid. From these beginnings kimch'i developed into a uniquely Korean traditional dish.

Early historical documents showed that vegetables fermented with salt from lactic acid, and the combination of salt and acid keep the vegetable from spoiling. Thus, kimch'i can be considered a processed food, preserved by the acidity formed from fermentation.

Koreans have been eating and enjoying kimch'i since tribal days. During the Three Kingdoms period, Koreans were said to make kimch'i with salt, draff from alcohol, *chang* (sauce), vinegar, and even the bark of elm. *Susuborichi kimch'i* was another period speciality, in which the vegetables were pickled with

Koreans have eaten kimch'i since the Three Kingdoms era (57 B.C.-A.D. 668). This mural from the Koguryŏ (37 B.C.-A.D. 668) Kingdom shows various kitchen utensils.

salt and rice powder.

The Koryŏ Dynasty saw the introduction of such delicacies as *mujang-atch'i* (Chinese radish preserved in soy sauce) and *musogumchŏli* (Chinese radish preserved in salt). Kimch'i made with the fruit of a Japanese pepper tree, water pepper, Japanese ginger and other spices was developed as well.

In the middle of the Chosŏn Dynasty, red pepper was brought to Korea for the first time, revolutionizing the way kimch'i was made within one generation. Before the advent of red pepper, kimch'i had been preserved in salt, vinegar, fennel and other spices. Around 1670, a popular kind of kimch'i was pickled gourd melon which was then salted. Another kind was made by packing leaf mustard into a small earthenware jar, over which warm water was poured, and setting the jar on a heated floor for ripening. This was an example of the *Mu-ch'im-chae* pickling method, in which the vegetable is fermented without salt. Another method was *saengch'i-ch'im-chae*. In this method, salted cucumbers would be peeled, chopped into 3 cm-length pieces, sliced thinly and dipped in water until the salt is diluted.

Garlic *chang-atchi*

Meanwhile, boiled pheasant meat would be minced and put in warm water together with the pickled cucumber, then salted to taste. This was served together with *napak-kimch'i*, which was fermented during the same time. Kimch'i culture had developed as such in the 1600s before the use of red pepper took hold.

Kimch'i of this period was made primarily from vegetables like gourd melon and cucumber. Cucumber kimch'i was especially popular, and was often sauteed in soy sauce and oil with pheasant meat.

By 1655, forms of kimch'i known as *ch'imgwajŏ* and *ch'imjupjŏ* had been developed. The former was made of eggplant, *chang* and wheat bran mixed together, then

Red peppers are one of the basic ingredients of kimch'i.

buried in warm manure for 20 days. This was the precursor to today's *chŭpchang*, a paste derived from soybean. Eggplant would be added to the *chŭpchang* to make eggplant *chang-atch'i*.

According to historical record, there were about eleven types of kimch'i by the end of the seventeenth century. Of course, there was no reference to red pepper as an ingredient of kimch'i at time, but Chinese radish, Chinese cabbage, gourd melon, bracken, and blue beans [*ch'ŏngt'ae-k'ong*], etc, are mentioned, as well as a description of how to make *tongch'imi*, pickled radish in salt water.

One kind of kimch'i at that time had radish immersed in a large quantity of water for four days. When the radish was purified of all oils, the liquid was discarded and the radish was put in a fresh batch of water. Spices were more commonly used for cucumber kimch'i. After being blanched in hot water, the cucumber was dried off and seasoned with salt, sugar, vinegar and other spices.

As late as 1715, red pepper was not yet an ingredient of kimch'i. Kimch'i was still being made as it always had been–salted and then pickled in vinegar–even one hundred years after the introduction of red pepper. Later, as records from the 1760s show, methods of pickling kimch'i became more diverse.

One new type of kimch'i was made by fermenting vegetables like radish, glue plant (an edible seaweed), squash and eggplant in red pepper, vinegar, mustard and other spices, and adding garlic juice. Another kind was made by slicing a cucumber lengthwise along three sides and stuffing it with red pepper flakes and garlic for ripening. Also, Chinese cabbage kimch'i, *tongch'imi*, Yongin cucumber kimch'i, winter eggplant kimch'i, abalone kimch'i, and oyster kimch'i among others were beginning to become an indispensable part of the Korean diet and lifestyle.

By the close of the 19th century the process of making kimch'i had considerably diversified and advanced, but kimch'i could still be categorized as of four kinds: *ŏmchangch'ae, chach'ae, chech'ae*, and *chŏch'ae*. The first kind refers to vegetables fermented in salt, draff, and spices for preservation for eating in winter. The second and fourth kinds are similar, but *chach'ae* is fermented in salt and rice, while *chŏch'ae* is pickled in fermented fish paste, chang, ginger, garlic, vinegar, etc. The taste of *chŏch'ae* is an intriguing blend of salty, sour and spicy flavors.

The first three kinds of kimch'i may be loosely regarded as types of *chŏch'ae*, but the latter is really a separate category in itself. How do they differ? Technically, *chŏch'ae* is eaten right after fermentation while *ŏmchangch'ae* is processed again, either by soaking in water or boiling in salty liquid. The difference between *chŏch'ae* and *chech'ae* is that the latter is pickled after being chopped and sliced, while the former is pickled in its original state.

Kimch'i fermented with *chŏtkal*, salted fish paste, was developed around this time. The usual vegetables like radish, cucumber and Chinese cabbage were fermented in seaweed, red pepper, ginger, vinegar and mustard of course, but to this was added clams, *chŏtkal*,

Recipe for kimch'i
1. Chinese cabbage is sliced and washed and then put into salt water.
2,3. Spices and thinly sliced vegetables such as Chinese radish or carrot are prepared.
4. The thinly sliced vegetables and spices are mixed.
5,6. The spiced vegetables are inserted into the cabbage leaves to make the kimch'i.

1

2

3

4

5

6

abalone, conch, squid, and other seafood. Abalone shell was added to cut the acidity, and then the mixture was salted to taste to produce lactic acid.

Korean kimch'i had almost fully evolved by this time. Subsequent developments included the use of fruit, meat and pine nuts and other variations, according to regional climate. Furthermore, ingredients changed as the quality of vegetables improved.

Nowadays, each region–indeed, each family–has its unique kind of kimch'i. Kimch'i indeed boasts many varieties, especially as the amount of red pepper and type of *chŏtkal* used vary from region to region.

From the cold northern provinces comes white kimch'i, *possam kimch'i* (Chinese cabbage stuffed with fish and many fruits vegetables), and *tongch'imi*, varieties that use less red pepper. The southwestern provinces are famed for their very spicy kimch'i, while the southeastern provinces are noted for their saltiness. Of the various kinds of *chŏtkal* used in kimch'i, the central and northern provinces relied on shrimp or clam *chŏtkal*, while southern provinces favored anchovy and hairtail *chŏtkal*.

But kimch'i is best known for its fiery hot red peppers. Red peppers are an excellent source of vitamin C, supplying 50 times as much apples do and twice as much as persimmons. Furthermore, the capsaicin that produces its hot taste is rich in vitamin E, which works with vitamin C as an antioxidant.

Thus, the Korean diet had in kimch'i a steady source of vitamins even during winter. What's more, the capsaicin kept the oils in *chŏtkal* from turning

Kimch'i is a staple food that is eaten every day

rancid and developing a fishy smell, while the combination of garlic and red pepper spurred the cultivation of lactic acid for fermentation.

Kimch'i is also a great source of fiber. Unrivalled in taste, appearance, and texture, it is also a source of both vegetable and animal nutrients and protein. Kimch'i is not merely a spicy accompaniment but a nutritious component of the meal indeed.

Depending on the type of kimch'i and the time of year it is eaten, there are several kinds of earthenware jars used for preparation and storage. Since kimch'i can only taste as it should if it is prepared with sincerity and devotion, even the jars had to be made in a certain way. The most solid and airtight jars, which kept the kimch'i from developing bad odors, were fired from clay dug up right after the first rainfall of spring , when the earth has just melted.

Kimch'i has to be carefully kept so it will not freeze or ferment further. Stored at 5 degrees Celsius, kimch'i can last four to six weeks. Traditionally, kimch'i jars were wrapped in straw and buried deep underground to keep the temperature constant. Also, it was necessary to prevent kimch'i from coming into contact with air to prevent if from going sour.

Today, new methods of preparing kimch'i have developed to reflect changes in growing seasons and lifestyle. Since vegetables can be cultivated year-round, Koreans are not as limited in their choice of ingredients. Furthermore, as more and more families opt to live in apartments in large cities, housewives no longer need to make kimch'i in such large quantities as in the past.

Each region and each family has its own unique varieties of Kimch'i.

Paech'u kimch'i

Kkaktugi

Ch'onggak kimch'i

Oisobaegi

Napak kimch'i made
on Cheju-do Island

Pyongyang-style
paech'u kimch'i

Nowadays, kimch'i factories mass produce various types of kimch'i and sell them around the world.

The Korean diet have in kimchi a steady source of vitamins even during winter. Kimchi is also a great source of fiber. Unrivalled in taste, appearance, and texture, it is also a source of both vegetable and animal nutrients and protein. Kimchi is not merely a spicy accompaniment but a nutritious component of the meal indeed.

Ssirŭm
Korean Wrestling

Ssirŭm, a Korean traditional art, is a type of folk competition in which two players, holding on to a satba (a cloth-sash tied around the waist), try to use their strength and various techniques to wrestle each other down to the ground.

Ssirŭm
Korean Wrestling

Ssirŭm, a Korean traditional form of wrestling, is a type of folk competition in which two players, holding on to a *satba* (a cloth-sash tied around the waist), try to use their strength and various techniques to wrestle each other down to the ground.

The history of *ssirŭm* began at the same time that communities began to form. In primitive societies, people unavoidably had to fight against wild beasts, not only for self-defense, but also to obtain food. In addition, it was impossible for these communities to avoid coming in conflict with other groups of different blood ties. As a result, people ended up practicing different forms of fighting to protect themselves. During this period, when grappling was a predominant method of combat, various wrestling techniques were born.

With the advancement of human intelligence and political and economic development among local communities in Korea, *ssirŭm* developed into a military

Ssirŭm is a form of Korean traditional wrestling
Competitors try their skills during folk competitions.

art. It can thus be said that *ssirŭm*'s elevated status as a military art was a natural outcome of social development.

By the beginning of the Koguryŏ Dynasty (37 B.C.-A.D.668), *ssirŭm* was already established as a military art. This is substantiated by the murals of Kakchŏch'ong (Tomb of the Wrestlers), which is believed to have been constructed in the 4th century. Drawn on a stone wall in the main chamber was a vivid scene depicting *ssirŭm*. The mural contains a scene showing two men wrestling, with a referee judging the match. The location of the drawing implies that *ssirŭm* was a major part of Korean lifestyle during that period.

Ssirŭm's status continued into the Koryŏ period

Ssirŭm gai[n]
widespread popula[r]
during the Chosŏn Dyna[sty]
"*Ssirŭm*," as depic[ted]
in a genre pict[ure]
by Kim Hong-[...]
Late Chosŏn Dyna[sty]
(rig[ht]

Ssirŭm as depicted
on a mural from
the Koguryŏ period
shows that *ssirŭm*
was a part of lifestyle.

(918-1392). A record in Koryŏsa (History of Koryŏ) states that in the mid-fourteenth century King Ch'unghye ordered soldiers to compete in *ssirŭm* and observed the match during a banquet. It was during the Chosŏn Dynasty (1392-1910), however, that *ssirŭm* gained increasingly widespread popularity.

Evidence of this is depicted in the genre pictures of Kim Hongdo, which frequently featured scenes of *ssirŭm* competitions; it is clear that by the Chosŏn era *ssirŭm* had become well-known as a folk competition in addition to being a traditional Korean military art.

Virtually every country has seasonal folk celebrations that contain the unique characteristics of that country, and Korea is no exception in this regard. *Ssirŭm* contests, which could be held virtually anywhere or at anytime, were a frequent part of the various celebrations held throughout the year. Many *ssirŭm* competitions occurred during *Tano* (the May Festival), but also during other holidays as well. On holidays such as the third day of the Third Moon, the eighth day of the Fourth Moon, Buddhist All Souls' Day during the Seventh Moon and the Harvest Moon Festival during the Eighth, townsfolk gathered to compete in *ssirŭm* matches as a way of sharing their joy and releasing mental and physical tensions from strenuous farming work that lasted from spring until fall.

The surrounding atmosphere became festive with the beginning of *ssirŭm* matches. On days when *ssirŭm* matches were held, gambling games such as *yut* (a four-stick game like parcheesi) and various card games, which were ordinarily prohibited, were allowed. Upon demonstration of a fine *ssirŭm* technique or announcement of the winner, the people would raise a shout of joy, and *nongak-nori* (farmers' music and dance) was performed.

Ssirŭm is performed on a *ssirŭmpan*, which refers to the grounds where *ssirŭm* matches are held. While the rise of *ssirŭm* as a modern sport has meant that *ssirŭmpans* are now prepared according to specific rules, there

The winner was customarily awarded a bull, a symbol of strength.

were no strict *ssirŭmpan* regulations in traditional folk competitions. A traditional *ssirŭmpan* was ordinarily prepared in a yard where many people could congregate, such as a large yard either outside a village entrance, where a zelkova tree could function as a pavilion, or inside the town. Preparation consisted simply of pouring sand in a circle over the *ssirŭm* ground. Posts were put up in four corners, and gold-colored strips were wrapped around the posts to prevent people from coming inside the ring. The reason for covering the *ssirŭmpan* with sand was to protect the wrestlers from injuries when they fell.

Ssirŭm practitioners were called *ssirŭmkun*. Among *ssirŭmkuns*, there were quite a few professionals who toured around the country for *ssirŭm* matches, and the better competitors obtained nationwide fame. It was considered quite an honor to be a *ssirŭmkun*, and the ability to compete with one's strength and ability in a *ssirŭm* match in the presence of congregated spectators was itself something to boast about.

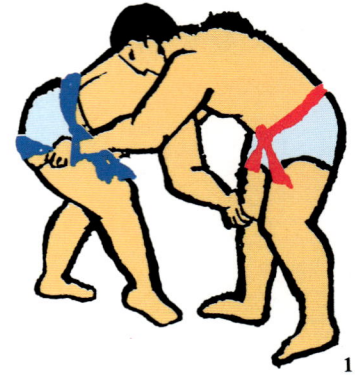

1

The final winner of the *ssirŭm* tournament was customarily awarded an ox, which was not only a symbol of strength, but also a valuable asset in an agricultural society. Because farming was primarily accomplished by an ox's strength at that time, it was a most meaningful and generous award in every respect.

In Korea today, *ssirŭm* has emerged as a sport in the limelight, rather than a mere traditional folk competition practiced only on holidays. Its popularity is such that matches are broadcast on television to enable people to watch from their homes.

Ssirŭm matches are held in group and individual matches. The competition schedule is determined by a drawing in the presence of the individual team's representative, while victory is determined by a player or a group's winning two out of three rounds of the match. Nonetheless, only one match determines a victory, depending on the circumstances of the match. The decision is made by the executive official after gathering opinions from the officials of the competition committee.

The *satba* has to be worn in a way such that a loop encircles the right leg and long waist strip is flexible enough not to be a hindrance during the match. The

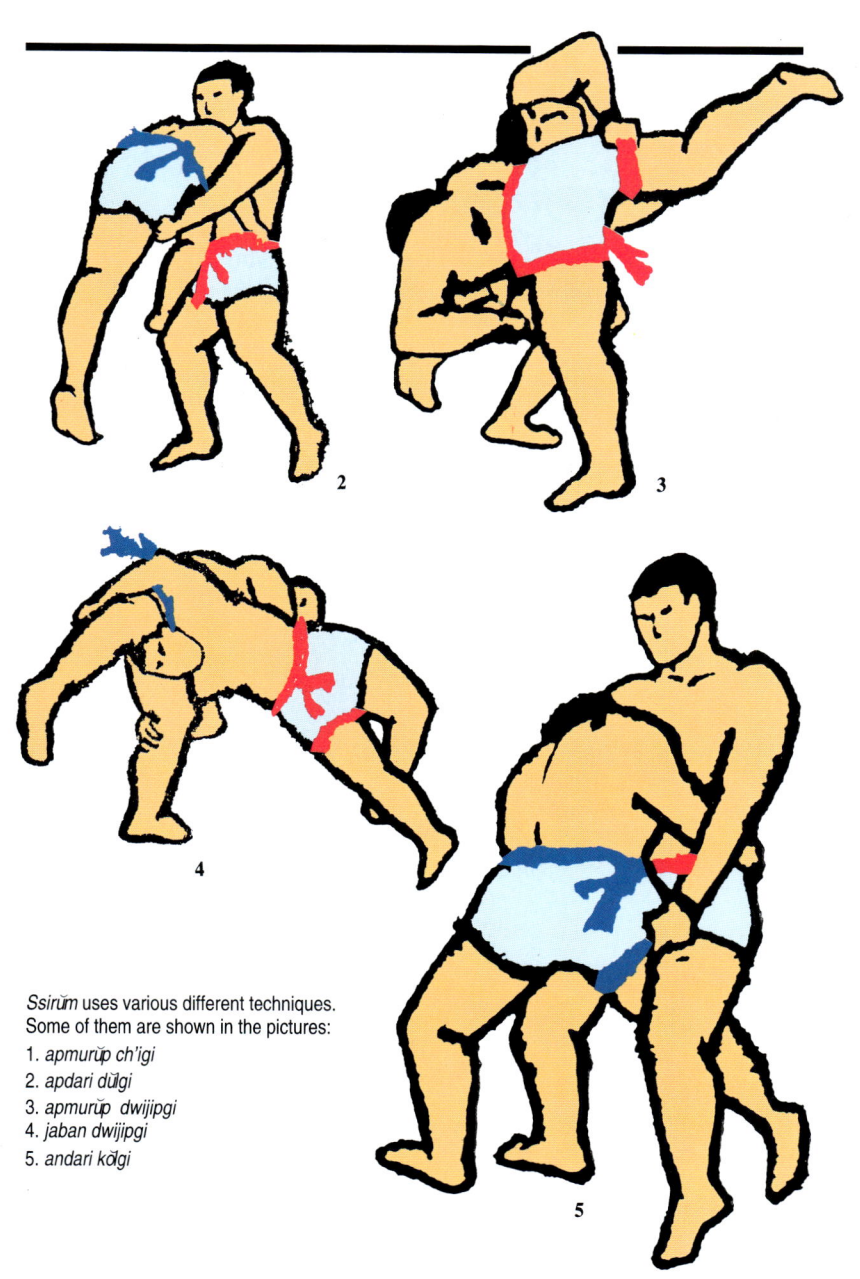

Ssirŭm uses various different techniques.
Some of them are shown in the pictures:

1. *apmurŭp ch'igi*
2. *apdari dŭlgi*
3. *apmurŭp dwijipgi*
4. *jaban dwijipgi*
5. *andari kŏlgi*

Grasp of *satba* plays an important role in *ssirŭm*.

juncture between the strip and the loop has to be along the central line of the right thigh. Prior to the match, the two players bow toward each other and the judge's stage, then sit down to grab the *satba*. Such etiquette stems from respect for the ways of *ssirŭm*. The two competitors kneel down on the floor, keeping a ten to thirty centimeter distance between their legs. They then lean their shoulder into each other simultaneously and grasp the *satba*. At that point, the player cannot step back with his right leg. Also, the *satba* cannot be held at a point beyond the mid-point of the right thigh or the waist. Upon completion of grasping the *satba*, the match begins with the signal of the referee.

When the *satba* is released by one of the players or a player is pushed outside the ring, a rematch is ordered. However, if one is pushed out intentionally or one hinders the opponent's holding the *satba*, a warning can be issued as a penalty. Two warnings become a citation; two citations result in the loss of a match; three citations result in the disqualification of a player. To enhance the player's spirit for the fight and to encourage him to perform his best, judging is determined by two wins out of three matches.

The time limit for the match differs according to category, which includes elementary, junior high school, and high school and above (including college and general public). A match for the elementary and junior high school categories is set for two minutes. If there is no winner, a two-minute extended round is held after one minute of rest. For matches in high school and higher categories, matches last for three minutes. If a winner is not decided, an extended match is held after a minute of rest.

Upon exhaustion of the second match time limit when the first match's winner has already been determined, the winner from the first match becomes the winner of the competition. If there is no winner during the first match, the winner from the second match wins. When the score after the first two rounds is 1-1 and a winner is not decided in the third round match due to expiration of the designated time limit, a player who has received a warning or citation loses the competition. If neither of the players has received a warning or citation, the person with the lighter body weight becomes the winner.

During the match, a player who touches the ground with any part of the body above the knee or steps out of the ring is defeated. If a player purposefully pushes his opponent outside the ring or steps outside due to his own mistake, a warning is given. However, when the match is completed outside the ring as a result of a player's natural progression in a *ssirŭm* move, the player whose move determined the end of the match becomes the winner. Squeezing the neck, hitting with the head, twisting the arms, kicking with the foot, punching with a fist, covering the eyes, and other actions that hinder the opponent's performance become grounds for revocation of the right to further participate in the competition.

The judging team consists of one chief referee and three sub-referees. In addition to judging the match, they are also responsible for administration of issues pertinent to match. The chief referee moves in and out of the ring and is expected to announce his judgments in a speedy and accurate fashion. Sub-referees are positioned outside the ring , one on the left and the other on the right. To ensure the fairness of the chief referee's decisions, sub-referees observe the match thoroughly. If an unfair judgment is announced or the chief referee is unable to make a decision upon completion of a match, they can request a revocation of the decision or a rematch. Sub-referees can also recommend the immediate cessation of the match when injury is likely to be incurred by a player due to the match itself or outside conditions.

The right combination of physical strength and advaned techniques is required in winning. The picture shows Lee Man-ki, the champion of the *Ch'ŏnhajangsa* the highest competition category in *ssirŭm* matches (right)

When progression of a match becomes impossible because of an accident during the match, a winner is determined by an agreement made between the chief and sub-referees. Absolute respect for the referees' authority is expected from the athletes, and they cannot challenge any judgments announced by either the chief referee or one agreed upon by both the chief and sub-

referees. When a challenge is raised by a sub-referee in regard to the chief referee's decision, or when judging by the chief referee alone becomes difficult, the sub-referee's opinions are incorporated into a final decision.

The chief referee announces the beginning and end of a match or the decision of a victory using a whistle. If any situation arises during the match that is likely to cause a player's injury or the *satba* is not held onto tightly, the chief referee may stop the match momentarily, signaling for the match to continue when the correction is made.

If a player does not appear in the ring after having been called three times by the chief referee, the player defaults the match. Any player who violates

the regulations of the match, uses violence or violent words, or demonstrates any improper behavior during the match can be immediately ordered to stop such behavior or be withdrawn from the ring.

For effective resolution of the issues related to the match, a penalty committee implements the decision made by the judging committee in relation to any incident that occurred or upon request for suspensions by various committees. If any unqualified player is found to be participating in the match, the player and the group that the player is affiliated with are disqualified. All results attained by that particular individual and the group are nullified, and a suspension notice is given out accoriding to regulations set forth by the penalty committee.

With the development of consistent rules and guidelines, *ssirŭm* has continued to progress from a traditional sport and self-defense method into a well-loved folk competition and popular modern sport that is a part of the lives of Koreans today.

Professional *ssirŭm* has become one of the most popular folk sports in Korea. Shown here is a modern *ssirŭmpan*.

The final winner of the ssirŭm
tournament was customarily
awarded a bull, which was not only
a symbol of strength, but also a
valuable asset in an agricultural
society.

Taekwondo

Taekwondo is an officially acknowledged international sport that originated in Korea and is today practiced worldwide. Taekwondo uses the whole body, particularly the hands and feet. It not only strengthens one's physique, but also cultivates character via physical and mental training. Coupled with techniques of discipline, taekwondo is a self defense martial art.

Taekwondo

T aekwondo is an officially acknowledged international sport that originated in Korea and is today practiced worldwide. Taekwondo uses the whole body, particularly the hands and feet. It not only strengthens one's physique, but also cultivates character via physical and mental training. Coupled with techniques of discipline, taekwondo is a self-defense martial art.

The evidence of taekwondo's existence as a systemized defense operation using the body's instinctive reflexes can be traced back to ceremonial games that were performed during religious events in the era of the ancient tribal states. During religious ceremonies such as Yŏnggo (a spirit-invoking drumming), Tongmaeng (a sort of thanksgiving ceremony in autumn), and Much'ŏn (Dance to Heaven), ancient Koreans performed a unique exercise for physical training. This exercise was the original inception of taekwondo.

Taekwondo is the only officially acknowledged international sport
to have originated in Korea. Exhibition by high-grade holders.

A *t'aekkyŏn* (an older name for taekwondo) match painted on a mural from the Koguryŏ (37 B.C.-A.D. 668) era.

With this historical background, taekwondo (also known by its older name, *t'aekkyŏn*) secured the status of Korean's traditional martial art. During the Three Kingdoms period, *t'aekkyŏn* became a required military art; the martial art was emphasized to enhance national defense and battle capabilities, and was practiced in the *Musadan* (a military organization) that was responsible for national defense.

Examples of *Musadan* are the *Sŏnbae* of Koguryŏ and the *Hwarang* of Shilla. *Sŏnbae*, which was founded during the era of King T'aejo of Koguryŏ, practiced *t'aekkyŏn* (also called *t'aekkoni*) to strengthen their country's defense capabilities. Strengthening this claim is a mural in the Muyong-ch'ong (Tomb of the Dancers) in southern Manchuria. Drawn on the ceiling of the burial chamber and the master chamber of the tomb was a vivid scene of a *t'aekkyŏn* match.

T'aekkyŏn was practiced in Shilla in order to reinforce national development, and was the basic martial art of the *Hwarang-do* (Flower of Youth Corps). Evidence attesting to *t'aekkyŏn*'s role during the Shilla period can be found in the Kŭmgang Yŏksasang (a guardian of a temple gate), which is now housed in the Kyŏngju National Museum.

The aforementioned traditions were continuously superseded and further developed during the Koryŏ period. The value of *t'aekkyŏn* as a martial art for the defense and prosperity of the nation was acknowledged, and as a consequence, its standards were raised, leading to further systemization and popularity. Among King Ŭijong's writings is a record stating that Yi Ŭimin was promoted because of his outstanding *t'aekkyŏn* techniques. The record also shows that Ch'oe Ch'unghŏn threw banquets and

One of the basic movements of *t'aekkyŏn* as shown by a Kŭmgang Yŏksasang (one of a pair of door guardians of a Buddhist temple) from the Shilla (57 B.C.-A.D. 935) period.

let strong men from the *Chungbang* (Council of Generals) compete against each other in *t'aekkyŏn* matches; winners from the match were awarded with government posts. Finally, there is a record about Pyŏn Anyŏl's winning matches against Im Kyŏnmi and Yŏm Hŭngbang and being promoted from assistant-head to head of the Royal Secretariat as a reward. Such evidence implies that the value of taekwondo as a martial art was acknowledged in the Koryŏ Dynasty at the national level, while also confirming the existence of clear judging criteria for competitions.

The basic movements of taekwondo are included in *Muye tobo t'ongji* (Comprehensive Illustrated Manual of Martial Arts), written during the Chosŏn (1392-1910) era.

Based on this information, it can be deduced that taekwondo, as a military art, had reached a level of high performance during the Koryŏ period. A number

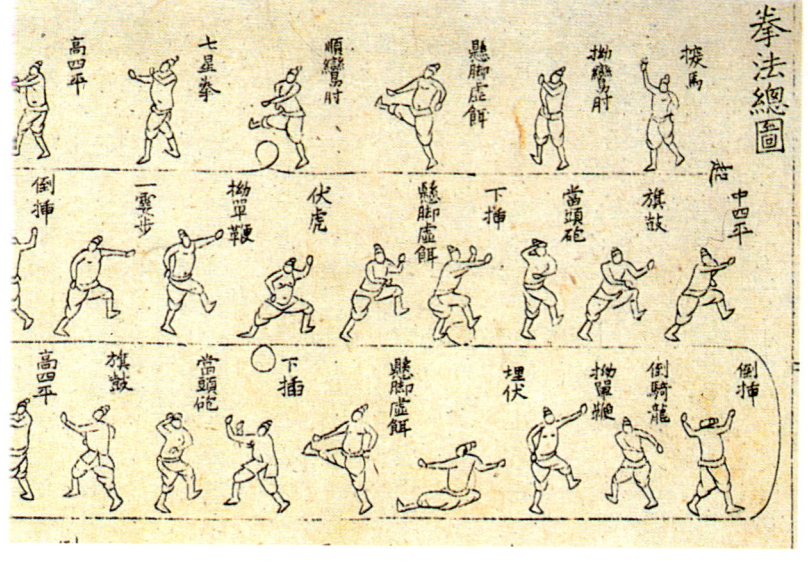

T'aekkyŏn and wrestling are depicted in this picture entitled *taek'waedo* (Portrait of Valor) by Yu Suk, a late Chosŏn era painter.

of written entries, such as "the rafter was moved when Yi Ŭimin hit the pillar with his bare fist," or "the wall was broken when Tu Kyŏngsŭng hit the wall with his fist" substantiate the high and sometimes lethal level of taekwondo standards at that time. Another record states, "Yi Ŭimin punched a man's backbone and killed him."

With the advent of explosives and the appearance of new weapons by the end of the Koryŏ era, however, taekwondo, which was highly supported at the national level during the beginning and middle periods of the Koryŏ Dynasty, received a steadily declining level of support. As a result of its weakened function as a martial art, the sport was transformed into a folk game at one point. According to records in the *Koryŏsa* (History of Koryŏ, 1454), people who gambled on *t'aekkyŏn* for money or material goods were punished by 100 strokes of a paddle; a house owner who provided boarding or gambling money to gamblers also received the same number of paddle beatings as punishment. Such records imply that *t'aekkyŏn* was enjoyed as a folk game by many people and was deeply rooted in Koreans' lives.

Later, during the Chosŏn era, military arts regained their prominence due to political circumstances in the early period of the dynasty's foundation and the need for national defense. People who were skilled in *t'aekkyŏn* received preferable treatment, and *t'aekkyŏn* was chosen as a military art. Documents show that during the selection of military soldiers by the Ŭihŭng-bu (a military command) during the 10th year of King T'aejong(1410), persons who had beaten three rivals in *t'aekkyŏn* matches were selected to become *pangp'aeguns* (shielding soldiers). In the following year, skills in *t'aekkyŏn* were applied as a major criterion for recruiting soldiers. This practice attracted to the military service many of the *kwanno*, male provincial government slaves, who by virtue of their work were mostly well versed in the martial art.

Once the country's organizational structure was solidified, nonetheless, the importance of the martial art was again deemphasized due to the unavoidable strengthening of the power of the literati. However, this trend was

Kyŏkp'a
(breaking boards)

Main techniques of taekwondo:

Arae-makki

Sonnal-ch'igi

Yŏpjirugi

Yŏpch'agi

Pandalch'agi

reversed when the country experienced severe difficulties such as the *Imjin waeran* (the Japanese invasion of Chosŏn) in 1592 and the *Pyŏngja horan* (the Manchu invasion) in 1636. At the national level, the *Hullyŏn togam* (Military Training Command) was established to support martial arts. *Muye tobo t'ongji*, a text for martial art, was written by Yi Tŏngmu and Pak Chega. Such national support enabled *t'aekkyŏn* to regain its vitality as a martial art and folk game.

In *Tongguk yŏji sungnam* (Augmented Survey of the Geography of Korea), it is stated that in one of the towns in Ŭnjin-hyŏn in Ch'ungch'ŏng-do province, people from the Ch'ungch'ŏng-do and Chŏlla-do provinces gathered around on Buddhist All Souls' Day to compete in *t'aekkyŏn* matches, while in the *p'ungsokhwa* (genre pictures) of that period scenes of *t'aekkyŏn* can often be found. Based on this evidence, it is clear that *t'aekkyŏn* was quite popular and deelpy rooted in the daily lives of Koreans.

With time's passage, methods of national defense changed, along with the liberalization of peoples' awareness. Consequently, *t'aekkyŏn* became primarily a folk match or game rather than a military art. With Japan's undisguised intention of invading Korea, however, *t'aekkyŏn* emerged as a national pastime. The fact that it was already established as a folk game, coupled with the Koreans' consciousness of being a homogeneous nation distinct from the Japanese, fueled their passion for the art.

During the period when Japan controlled Korea,

Taekwondo is now firmly established as an international sport.

t'aekkyŏn was suppressed. Nevertheless, it was secretly passed on among certain *t'aekkyŏn* masters even during this period.

After national independence in 1945, *t'aekkyŏn's* revitalization began once again, aided by restored personal freedoms. It was during this period that a new word, *"t'aekwon,"* was coined and began to be widely used. Concurrently, the characteristics of the master-trainee relationship in taekwondo changed to emphasize the characteristics of taekwondo as more of a sport than a martial art. With the foundation of the Korea Taekwondo Association in September of 1961, taekwondo officially became a sport entry.

In 1962, the Korea Taekwondo Association became a member organization of the Korea Amateur Sports Association, and the following year taekwondo was chosen as a regular entry for the National Sports Festival. In 1971 taekwondo's outstanding value was acknowledged, and taekwondo was recognized as a national sport; today there are about 3,700 taekwondo practice halls and approximately 10,000 masters in Korea, along with 3,000,000 grade-holders and 3,500,000 trainees.

In 1971, the Korea Taekwondo Association established etiquette criteria to guide those practicing taekwondo. The criteria include the areas of etiquette and attitude, articles to follow in daily living places and in practice halls, dress manner and personal appearance guidelines to be followed when conversing or visiting someone. The Kukkiwon was opened in 1972 to function as the central practice hall and competition stadium for taekwondo.

The first World Taekwondo Championship was held in Seoul during 1973, at which time the World Taekwondo Federation was founded. The World Taekwondo Federation eventually became a member of the GAISF(General Association of International Sports Federations), and was chosen as an official entry by the committee for the International Soldiers Meet (CISM) in 1976. Today the World Taekwondo Federation has 132 member countries, and 3,000 masters have been dispatched to these countries to instruct approximately 40,000,000 trainees worldwide.

The sport's steady progress and growth were responsible for taekwondo's selection as a demonstration sport for the Olympic Games at the General Assembly of the International Olympic Committee on July 15, 1980. During the General Assembly of the International Olympic Committee in 1981, taekwondo was also chosen for inclusion in the 10th Asian Games. Having been selected as a demonstration sport for the 1988 Olympic Games, taekwondo firmly established its presence in the international sports arena.

The First International Taekwondo Academic Conference, which was held in Seoul in December 1983, was another event which greatly contributed to the development of taekwondo. Partially as a result of the heightened worldwide interest in taekwondo demonstrated by this event, it was decided during the International Olympic Committee meeting held in Sydney, Australia, that taekwondo would be an official

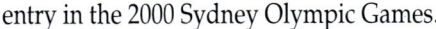

entry in the 2000 Sydney Olympic Games.

The training methods of taekwondo can be differentiated into *kibon tongjak*, *p'umsae*, *kyŏrugi*, *tallyŏn*, and *hoshinsul*. The *kibon tongjak* (basic movements) refer to dynamic elements of the use of hands and feet and are the basis of taekwondo. They include *ch'igi* (striking) techniques by use of fists and the outer side of the hand. *P'umsae* refers to training that is done alone with an imaginary counterpart. Following the drill line, one practices to master effective techniques of attack and defense movements so as to improve one's readiness, muscular power, flexibility, ability to shift one's center of power, control of breathing, and speed of movement. Types of *p'umsae* include *T'aeguk* (1-8 chang) and *P'alkwae* (1-8 chang) for non-grade-holders, and *Koryŏ Kŭmgang*, *T'aebaek*, *P'yŏngwŏn*, *Shipjin*, *Chit'ae*, *Ch'ŏnkwŏn*, *Hansu*, and *Ilyŏ* for grade-holders.

Kyŏrugi, an application of *P'umsae* to an actual situation in order to demonstrate techniques of attack and defense, is divided into two parts: *mach'uŏ kyŏrugi* and *kyŏrugi*. *Mach'uŏ kyŏrugi* refers to a synchronized demonstration of given attack and defense techniques, while *kyŏrugi* refers to the free application of those techniques to an opponent's vulnerable areas. The latter enhances one's spirit of fighting and courage.

Tallyŏn involves strengthening body parts such as one's hands and feet, through the use of various equipment, in order to increase one's power for attack and defense, while *hoshinsul* consists of techniques to

Nop'ich'agi (high kick)

defeat a rival's attack and effectively counterattack.

Taekwondo matches are held according to weight categories. These categories include pinweight, flyweight, bantamweight, featherweight, welterweight, middleweight, and heavyweight. The time allotted for a match is three three-minute rounds, with a one minute rest between rounds.

The competition floor is a square with sides of a total length of eight meters. A mattress is placed on the floor. For the safety of the competitor, protective pads for certain parts of the body, such as the torso and head, are worn over the competition outfit. Judging is carried out by one examiner, one chief referee, and four sub-referees.

The power and grace of taekwondo was demonstrated during the opening ceremony of the 1988 Olympic Games in Seoul.

The evidence of taekwondo's existence as a systemized defence operation using the body's instinctive reflexes can be traced back to ceremonial games that were performed during religious events in the era of the ancient tribal states.

Gardens

orean gardens simulate the natural landscape with hills, streams and fields. They
e usually small in scale, but have an ideal harmony of nature and man. The
incipal idea is to blend the structures into nature with the least possible
sturbance of the environment, because, in the Korean mind, nature is already a
rfect and an absolute entity that regenerates and sustains life. In the long tradition
garden making in Korea, adding man-made elements to the purest of spaces is
nsidered a violation and something to be approached with utmost care and
servation.

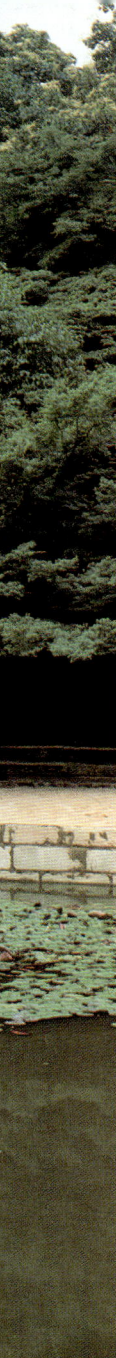

Gardens

Korean gardens simulate the natural landscape with hills, streams and fields. They are usually small in scale, but have an ideal harmony of nature and man. The prinicipal idea is to blend the structures into nature with the least possible disturbance of the environment, because, in Korean mind, nature is already a perfect and an absolute entity that regenerates and sustains life.

In the long tradition of garden making in Korea, adding man-made elements to the purest of spaces is considered a violation and something to be approached with utmost care and reservation. The essential idea behind the Korean art of garden building is to make it look more natural than nature itself. In many cases, what appears to be the work of nature turns out, at a closer look, to be the result of very conscious efforts. Korean gardens are characterized by a submission to nature in an attempt to attain beauty and function.

Korea has developed a unique garden culture during its long history. This is *puyongchŏng* located in Ch'angdŏkkung Palace in Seoul.

Korea has a long history of gardens. The oldest records date to the Three Kingdoms period (57B.C.-A.D.668) when architecture showed notable development. An important early history of the Korean nation, *Samguk sagi* (History of the Three Kingdoms) provides numerous pieces of evidence of royal palace gardens.

The earliest record of a garden in the book is attributed to the Koguryŏ Kingdom (37B.C.-A.D.668). It says that in the sixth year of the regin of King Tongmyŏng, the founder of Koguryŏ, mysterious peacocks swarmed into the courtyard of the royal palace. In the second year of reign of King Changsu (A.D.414), the same source claims that curious birds flocked into the royal palace, another indication that the palace had a garden to attract such birds.

The book implies that Paekche(18B.C.-A.D.660) had gardens of higher aesthetical standards by saying that, during the reign of King Mu (r.600-640), a pond was made to the south of the royal palace with the source of water supply located 8km away. Willow trees were planted along all four banks of the pond, which had in the center a miniature island named after a legendary mountain in China where Taoist immortals were said to dwell. Remains of the pond are found today in Puyŏ, the old capital of Paekche. It is called *Kungnamji*, or the Pond South of the palace.

There is also the record that in 655, King Uija had the palace of the crown prince extensively renovated and a pavilion named *Manghaejŏng*, or the Sea Watching Pavilion, built to the south of his palace. The

Kungnamji, located in Puyŏ, the old capital of Paekche.

sea here is assumed to have meant the *Kungnamji* Pond surrounded by willow trees, located to the south of the main palace.

In Shilla (57B.C.-A.D.935), the founding monarch Pak Hyŏkkŏse built a palace in the capital city of Kŭmsŏng, which is today's Kyŏngju, in 32 B.C., according to the History of the Three Kingdoms. The book also says that, during the reign of Ch'ŏmhae Isagum(r.247-284), a dragon appeared from a pond located to the east of the royal palace, and willow trees that lay to the south of the capical city rose by themselves.

The best preserved among all ancient palace gardens is *Anapchi* Pond in Kyŏngju, which was recently drained for an excavation and restoration.

Built as part of the detached palace of the crown prince
during the reign of King Munmu (r.661-681), the
artificial pond had five buildings along its shore
stretching 1,330 meters, each situated to command a
full view of the pond. Of the five, three pavilion-like
structures have been restored.

Anapchi has curved embankments on the northern

and eastern sides, somewhat resembling the coastiline
of a ria. The southern end is perfectly straight while the
western side is angular. All of the four sides are lined
with dressed stones. In the middle of the pond are
three small islands alluding to Taoist sanctuaries.

In an entry dated A.D. 674, the History of the Three
Kingdoms records that "a pond was made with

mountain-islands, flowering plants were grown, and rare birds and strange animals were raised in the palace." It is believed that plants such as orchids, peonies, lotus and azaleas, and birds and animals like swans, peacocks and deer were kept in the palace. On the shore and around the islands are simulated beaches made of rocks.

When *Anapchi* was drained and excavated in 1975, many relics dating from the Unified Shilla period (668-935) were found. They included a wooden frame which is believed to have been designed to grow lotus in a limited area in the pond. The entire floor of the pond was covered with pebbles to keep the water clear. On the whole, *Anapchi* and the surrounding garden were designed in a microcosmic style to symbolize the dwellings of Taoist fairies. The entire area was so arranged as to create the effect of a landscape painting.

Another important Shilla garden in Kyŏngju is the one at the site of a detached palace in the southern valley of Mt. Namsan. At the site of its *P'osŏkchŏng* Pavilion, believed to have been built in the eight century, is a water channel in which wine cups floated around during royal

One of the most famous gardens during the Unified Shilla period was *P'osŏkchŏng*, where poetry and music could always be heard.

Fantastically shaped rocks were placed around the pavilion to give elegance to the garden (left).

feasts. The channel defines an abalone-shaped area. The garden seems to have been a lovely sight with thick bamboo groves, beautiful streams and dense woods of pine and zelkova trees.

During Koryŏ (918-1392), the pleasure-seeking Ŭijong had various beautiful pavilions constructed in a royal villa in 1157 as part of a project to build a simulated fairyland. He ordered one of the pavilions to be covered with fine celadon roof tiles, which was criticized as an excessive luxury by offcials.

The art of garden making in the Chosŏn period

(1392-1910) is best exemplified by the Huwon of Ch'angdŏkkung Palace in Seoul. Comprising some 300,000 square meters of the entire 405,636 square meters of the palace property, the garden is tastefully laid out with picturesque pavilions and halls, lotus ponds, fantastically shaped rocks, stone bridges, stairways, water troughs and springs scattered among dense woods, all essential elements of a traditional

Stone materials are the most notable features in Korean-style gardens. *Okryuch'ŏn* at the Huwon in Ch'angdŏkkung Palace (above).

Chuhamru of the Huwon where lotus flowers were planted in stone water holders (left).

Korean-style garden.

Amisan Garden in the back of *Kyot'aejŏn*, once the royal bedchamber of Kyŏngbokkung palace, provides another attractive example of Chosŏn palatial gardens. It has four brick chimneys adorned with beautiful patterns, stone water holders and fantastic rocks placed among the plants on the terraced flower beds.

Not far from *Amisan* Garden, in the northern section of the palace, a two-story hexagonal pavilion named *Hyang-Wŏnjŏng* stands in the middle of a lotus pond. A beautiful wooden bridge spans the pond to the pavilion.

In Tamyang, located in Korea's southwestern Chŏl-lanam-do province, a woodland garden of a 16th

Korean gardens allow visitors to enjoy nature as it is. *Soswaewon* at Tamyang-gun in Chŏllanam-do province (above).
Garden seen from *Hwallaechŏng* pavilion at *Sŏn'gyochang* in Kangnŭng (right).

century nobleman scholar, named Soswaewŏn, or the Garden of Pure Mind, offers a fine example of Chosŏn literati gardens combining Confucian idealism and Taoist naturalism. Approached by a long, arched gateway of a thick bamboo grove, the garden has a rapid stream burbling down a rocky valley by pavilions, a lotus pond and a water mill. It is adorned with a variety of trees and shrubs including paulownias, plums, pine trees, maples, plantains, gingko trees, orchids, chrysanthemums and lotuses-all favorite plants among ancient Koreans for both their appearances and symbolic meanings. The idyllic atmosphere of the place inspired many writers and poets.

In Kangnung, Kangwŏn-do province, near the east

coast, *Sŏn-gyŏjang*, or the Mansion of Ferry Bridge, maintains much of the stylishness of the Chosŏn upper-class home garden of the early 19th century. The mansion is comprised of the outer quarters for the men of the family, the inner quarters for women and childern, and the servant quarters, each surrounded with low stone walls with little landscaping. There is a square lotus pond near the entrance, with a pavilion perched on the shore and a miniature mountain-island in the center, in a style reminiscent of a lotus pond in the Huwon in Seoul.

A lotus is one of the most important structures in Korean garden. *Hyang-wonchŏng.*

Korean gardens are characterized by c submission to nature in an attempt to attain beauty and function.